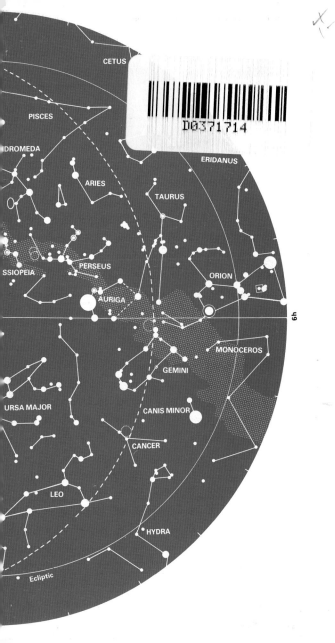

An Instant Guide to
STARS &
PLANETS

The sky at night
described and illustrated in full color

PAMELA FOREY AND
CECILIA FITZSIMONS
CONSULTANT EDITOR
IAN RIDPATH

GRAMERCY BOOKS
NEW YORK

Key to magnitudes and other symbols used in constellations

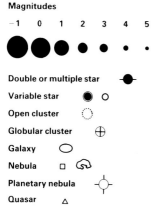

Magnitudes

| −1 | 0 | 1 | 2 | 3 | 4 | 5 |

Double or multiple star

Variable star

Open cluster

Globular cluster

Galaxy

Nebula

Planetary nebula

Quasar

Copyright © 1988 by Atlantis Publications Ltd.
All rights reserved under International and Pan-American
Copyright Conventions.

No part of this book may be reproduced or transmitted in any form or
by any means electronic or mechanical including photocopying,
recording, or by any information storage and retrieval system, without
permission in writing from the publisher.

This 1999 edition is published by Gramercy Books™
an imprint of Random House Value Publishing, Inc.,
201 East 50th Street, New York, New York 10022.

Gramercy Books™ and colophon are trademarks of
Random House Value Publishing, Inc.

Random House
New York • Toronto • London • Sydney • Auckland
http://www.randomhouse.com/

Printed and bound in Malaysia

A CIP catalog record for this book is available
from the Library of Congress.

ISBN 0-517-63549-6

15 14 13

Contents

Introduction

The night sky can be a brilliant and breathtaking sight. The Moon may be so bright it lights up the sky and bathes the Earth in its soft mysterious glow. But at the dark of the Moon, the night becomes more wonderful, with the Milky Way stretching across the heavens and myriads of stars twinkling brightly in the darkness.

Sometimes, on a very dark night, it feels as if you can stretch up and touch the stars, they seem so close. But the reality of the distances involved defies the imagination. The Big Dipper is the pattern of stars that everyone is most familiar with; the closest of the seven stars that make up this constellation is 60 light years away. The star is so far away that the light we see shining today left the star 60 years ago. And this star is not very far away as stars go.

Men have been trying to make sense of the night sky, to fit the stars into patterns and to understand their nature, since the earliest civilizations. It is really only in the last 100 years that we have finally begun to make sense of the Universe. This book describes the various elements that go into the making of the Universe, the galaxies, the nebulae and star clusters, and the natures of the stars themselves. It describes the constellations, the patterns of stars that men have seen in the sky, and the Solar System in which we live, with its Sun and nine planets. The book not only acts as a simple guide to the constellations and the planets but gives you the background information that you need to make sense of the sky as well.

How to use this book

The book is divided into four sections, **The Structure of the Universe**, **Star Charts**, **the Constellations** and **the Solar System**. Each section is indicated by a different color band at the top of each page together with an identification symbol. In the section on the Structure of the Universe, the nature of galaxies, nebulae and stars is explained; in the section on Star Charts, guidance is given on how to find the major constellations in the sky; in Constellations, illustrations and details are given on the major constellations of the northern hemisphere; the section on the Solar System includes the latest information on our neighboring planets and their moons, brought back by the Voyager and Mariner missions.

The Structure of the Universe

This section provides the background information necessary to the understanding of what we see in the night sky. It explains stars; star types and the birth and life of a star; nebulae and clusters; pulsars and quasars; galaxies and globular clusters. It provides examples of each and also gives cross references to the constellations so that the reader can locate and see the examples for himself. The section also functions as a kind of additional extension of the glossary for the rest of the book.

Star charts

At the end of the section on the Structure of the Universe there are three pages explaining why the constellations change with time of night and with the seasons. With this in mind, the section goes on to explain how to use the star charts. These are eight pages of seasonal maps designed to help you locate the constellations in the sky at any time of year.

The Constellations

This section gives details of the major constellations seen in the night sky in the northern hemisphere, north of 30° North. Location details in the text, used with the key constellation inset into the illustration, together with the section on star charts and the sky maps in the endpapers, help you to locate each one in the sky.

Each constellation is illustrated and details are provided of features of interest, including double and variable stars, galaxies, nebulae and clusters. A key to the magnitude of the stars and to other symbols in the illustrations is given on page 6.

Fig. 1 Key to Fact Panel

Example: α (Polaris), yellow supergiant. mag. 2.1, 700 l.y.

α Each major star of a constellation is designated by a letter of the Greek Alphabet (see Naming the Stars, page 11).

Polaris. Some well-known stars, like this one, are given common names. These have been included where relevant.

Yellow supergiant. Star type of star (see pages 18–19).

mag. 2.1. The magnitude of the star (see page 12).

700 l.y. The distance away of the star in light years (see page 12).

There is also a fact panel with information on the major stars which form the constellation (see Fig. 1).

The Solar System

This section gives details of our Solar System and how we think it was formed; on the structure of the Sun and how it works, on the corona, prominences and flares; on the planets and their moons. For each planet, details are given on its orbit and position with regard to the Sun, on its surface features (where relevant) and atmosphere.

Now you are ready to use this book. It fits into your pocket so take it with you (together with a small pocket torch and your binoculars) next time you are out after dark. Or keep it in the car. Or use it in your back yard. Happy starwatching!

Fig. 2 Specimen Page (Constellation)

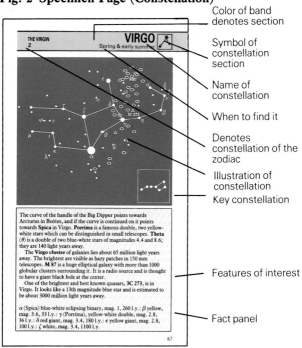

Color of band denotes section

Symbol of constellation section

Name of constellation

When to find it

Denotes constellation of the zodiac

Illustration of constellation

Key constellation

Features of interest

Fact panel

THE VIRGIN
Z

VIRGO
Spring & early summer

The curve of the handle of the Big Dipper points towards Arcturus in Boötes, and if the curve is continued on it points towards **Spica** in Virgo. **Porrima** is a famous double, two yellow-white stars which can be distinguished in small telescopes. **Theta** (θ) is a double of two blue-white stars of magnitudes 4.4 and 8.6; they are 140 light years away.
 The **Virgo cluster** of galaxies lies about 65 million light years away. The brightest are visible as hazy patches in 150 mm telescopes. **M 87** is a huge elliptical galaxy with more than 1000 globular clusters surrounding it. It is a radio source and is thought to have a giant black hole at the center.
 One of the brightest and best known quasars, **3C 273**, is in Virgo. It looks like a 13th magnitude blue star and is estimated to be about 3000 million light years away.

α (Spica) blue-white eclipsing binary, mag. 1, 260 l.y.: β yellow, mag. 3.6, 33 l.y.: γ (Porrima), yellow-white double, mag. 2.8, 36 l.y.: δ red giant, mag. 3.4, 180 l.y.: ε yellow giant, mag. 2.8, 100 l.y.: ζ white, mag. 3.4, 1100 l.y.

67

10

Viewing the Stars

You can see up to 4000 stars with the naked eye on a good night, when there is no Moon and the air is really clear. That is why a frosty winter's night provides such good star watching conditions. With a pair of binoculars you can see far more stars and can pick up their colors, as well as seeing nebulae, clusters and galaxies. **Binoculars** are categorized by their degree of magnification and their lens aperture. Thus binoculars rated 7×40, 8×30 and 10×50 have progressively higher powers of magnification (the first figure) and catch varying amounts of light (the second figure). The lens aperture (the second figure) determines the field of view and the clarity of the image. These are all good binoculars for astronomical purposes. Magnification of more than $\times 10$ is impracticable since the hands are not steady enough to keep such a highly magnified image still.

For a general view of the sky binoculars are unbeatable and they are relatively inexpensive. However if you see an interesting object like a globular cluster or nebula, you may want to examine it at a higher magnification. For this you need an amateur **telescope** mounted on a good tripod to give it steadiness. Most amateur telescopes have an aperture of 50–60 mm and usually provide a magnification of about $\times 100$. For more serious study, telescopes of 75 mm or 150 mm aperture would be needed. Telescopes are usually mounted on an altazimuth tripod which gives movement in both the vertical and the horizontal planes.

Naming the Stars

Bright stars are given double names, the first part being a letter of the Greek alphabet, and the second the possessive name of the constellation to which it belongs. An example would be Alpha Centauri, the closest star to our Sun which is found in the constellation Centaurus. Generally the Alpha star of a constellation is the brightest, the Beta star the second brightest and so on. But this rule does not always hold true because some of the stars were named inaccurately, some have changed in magnitude and some of the constellations have also been changed. Fainter stars may be given Roman letters or numbers. The Greek alphabet is given in Table 1, for reference.

Objects in the sky other than stars are given Messier (M) numbers, from the catalogue compiled by Messier in the 18th century or NGC numbers from the much more comprehensive New General Catalogue compiled in the 19th century.

Table 1. Greek alphabet

α	Alpha	ι	Iota	ρ	Rho
β	Beta	κ	Kappa	σ	Sigma
γ	Gamma	λ	Lambda	τ	Tau
δ	Delta	μ	Mu	υ	Upsilon
ϵ	Epsilon	ν	Nu	φ	Phi
ζ	Zeta	ξ	Xi	χ	Chi
η	Eta	o	Omicron	ψ	Psi
θ	Theta	π	Pi	ω	Omega

Glossary

Aphelion and **Perihelion**. The orbits of most of the planets around the Sun are eccentric, ie not circular. The planet approaches to its closest point from the Sun at perihelion (1) and reaches its furthest point at aphelion (2).

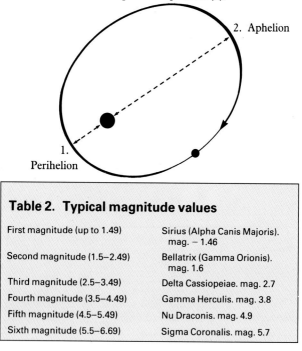

2. Aphelion

1. Perihelion

Table 2. Typical magnitude values

First magnitude (up to 1.49)	Sirius (Alpha Canis Majoris). mag. − 1.46
Second magnitude (1.5–2.49)	Bellatrix (Gamma Orionis). mag. 1.6
Third magnitude (2.5–3.49)	Delta Cassiopeiae. mag. 2.7
Fourth magnitude (3.5–4.49)	Gamma Herculis. mag. 3.8
Fifth magnitude (4.5–5.49)	Nu Draconis. mag. 4.9
Sixth magnitude (5.5–6.69)	Sigma Coronalis. mag. 5.7

Light year. The distance travelled by light in one year, about 6 million million miles.

Magnitude. The brightness of a star. In Greek times stars were classed from first to sixth magnitude, first magnitude stars being the brightest and sixth magnitude the faintest visible to the naked eye. This system has now been put on a mathematical basis. A first magnitude star is 2½ times brighter than a second magnitude star which is 2½ times brighter than a third magnitude star and so on. A first magnitude star is 100 times brighter than a sixth magnitude star. The scale thus formed is logarithmic. The scale can be extended indefinitely in either direction, for example Sirius, the brightest star in the sky has a negative value for its magnitude (-1.46) and the Sun's magnitude is -26.8. At the other end of the scale, the faintest objects which have been detected have a magnitude of about 24. Typical magnitudes are shown in Table 2 and the ten brightest stars in the sky are shown in Table 3.

These magnitudes are all apparent magnitudes, since they depend not only on the star's actual brightness but also on its distance away. Apparent magnitude may bear little relation to a star's real brightness, known as its absolute magnitude.

Table 3. Brightest Stars in the Sky

Star	Constellation	Mag.	Star Type	Distance
Sirius	Canis Major	-1.46	White	8.6 l.y.
Canopus	Carina	-0.72	White supergiant	1200 l.y.
Alpha Centauri	Centaurus	-0.27	Yellow double	4.3 l.y.
Arcturus	Boötes	-0.04	Red giant	36 l.y.
Vega	Lyra	0.03	Blue-white	26 l.y.
Capella	Auriga	0.08	Yellow double	42 l.y.
Rigel	Orion	0.1	Blue-white supergiant	910 l.y.
Procyon	Canis Minor	0.38	Yellow white	11.3 l.y.
Achernar	Eridanus	0.5	Blue-white	85 l.y.
Betelgeuse	Orion	0.4–1.3	Red supergiant	310 l.y.

The Structure of the Universe

We do not know how the universe began but we do know that it is expanding and that it reaches beyond our ability to see, even with the most sophisticated equipment. The universe contains countless galaxies, all becoming further and further apart as the universe continues to expand, receding from each other at thousands or hundreds of thousands of miles a second. Those furthest away from us are receding fastest.

Galaxies

Galaxies are formed of stars together with interstellar clouds of dust and gas (nebulae) and vast areas of space. They are rotating in space and many become spiral in form as a result, with a dense oval central bulge and trailing arms. In the arms are concentrated the dust and gas clouds, the nebulae, in which active star formation is occurring. A typical spiral galaxy contains 100,000 million stars and measures 100,000 light years in diameter. It also has a galactic halo which contains gas and dust, individual stars and globular clusters. Associated with these large spiral galaxies are often smaller non-spiral galaxies, like the two satellite galaxies found with the Andromeda Galaxy. Elliptical galaxies are generally older, with many red giant stars; they contain few interstellar dust and gas clouds, and star formation has virtually ceased.

Galaxies are grouped in clusters, for example our own Galaxy, the Milky Way, is part of a local cluster of galaxies travelling together in space. It contains several large galaxies and about 20 smaller satellite systems. Some galaxy clusters are much larger than our local group, for instance the Virgo cluster contains about a thousand galaxies. One of these (M 87) is a "supergalaxy," a giant elliptical system with a massive black hole at its center.

Quasars

Quasars, like 3C 345 in Hercules, are very remote, very luminous objects which emit X-rays. 3C 345 is one of the closest quasars, 8,000 million light years away and a 16th magnitude light source even at that distance, but it can only be seen in large telescopes. The furthest quasar yet found is more than 13,000 million light years away and is receding from us at about 90% of the speed of light. Quasars are quite small, in comparison to a galaxy. Their light is thought to come from the energy emitted by clouds of gas as it was pulled into black holes at the centers of galaxies.

The Milky Way, which is the galaxy that contains our Solar System, can be seen on dark nights as a glowing band of stars and nebulae stretching across the sky. The Sun lies in a spiral arm of the galaxy, about 30,000 light years from its center, and what we can see is the central bulge of the galaxy, lying edge on to our field of view.

The Milky Way contains about 100,000 million stars and measures about 100,000 light years in diameter. It has two smaller satellite galaxies associated with it, the Magellanic Clouds, which can only be seen from the southern hemisphere, in the constellations of Dorado and Tucana. The Clouds look like separate pieces of the Milky Way. The Large Magellanic Cloud contains about 10,000 million stars, the Small Magellanic Cloud 500 million stars; the Large Cloud lies about 160,000 light years away, the Small Cloud about 190,000 light years away.

15

The Andromeda Galaxy in the constellation of Andromeda, at 2.2 million light years away, is the closest spiral galaxy to our own and the only one visible to the naked eye, apart from the Milky Way and the Magellanic Clouds. It is a member of our Local Cluster and best seen in low power telescopes or as prints of long exposure photographs. It occupies an area of the sky five times the apparent diameter of the full Moon, has a diameter of about 150,000 light years and contains around 300,000 million stars. It is accompanied by two small satellite galaxies, M 32 and NGC 205, both visible in small telescopes.

The Andromeda Galaxy is the largest of the galaxies in the Local Cluster and the Milky Way is the next largest. The Triangulum Galaxy, which lies 2.35 million light years away in the small constellation of Triangulum, between Andromeda and Aries, is smaller with only 10,000 million stars. It forms a much looser spiral than the Milky Way and is visible in binoculars or with a small telescope.

GLOBULAR CLUSTERS

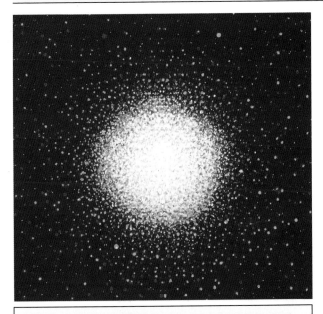

Globular clusters are spherical clusters of stars bound together by gravity. More than a hundred are known in the Milky Way where they pursue eccentric inclined orbits in the galactic halo. The nearest is more than 8000 light years away.

Sagittarius is a good constellation to examine for globular clusters, with M 22 being one of the finest, ranked second only to Omega Centauri and 47 Tucanae, both visible in the southern hemisphere. To the naked eye these three clusters appear like hazy stars, their true nature becoming apparent only in telescopes. M 13 is a giant cluster in Hercules with about 300,000 stars; it is just visible to the naked eye but is better viewed through binoculars or a small telescope.

A typical globular cluster measures about 150 light years across and contains about 100,000 stars, although a large cluster may contain up to a million stars. They are quite old, containing many red giant stars of the RR Lyrae variable type. In the center of a globular cluster the stars are dense and only light days apart, instead of light years.

Stars

Stars are high temperature balls of hydrogen and helium, so hot that nuclear fusion reactions occur in their cores. Our Sun is a star. There are many different types of stars, varying from cool dim red dwarfs to superhot superluminous blue giants. The type to which a star belongs depends on its mass, its size, its temperature, its color and its magnitude. Stars in their prime are classed as main sequence stars or dwarfs (white dwarfs are exceptions to this rule, see below); giants (old expanded stars resulting from red or yellow dwarf stars); or supergiants (old expanded stars resulting from massive blue or white stars).

Stars range in mass from about one tenth the mass of our Sun to about 30 times its mass. Mass is a measurement of the matter contained in the star. Stars vary considerably more in size than they do in mass. White dwarf stars may only be the size of our Earth but contain as much mass as our Sun — they are very dense. Giant stars may contain only ten times the mass of our Sun but measure several hundred times its diameter. The matter in these stars is much more diffuse. Supergiants are even larger and more massive.

The brightness of a star (its magnitude) depends on its surface temperature, as does its color. Blue and white stars are the hottest and brightest, with a temperature of 11,000–45,000 °F. Yellow and red stars are cooler and dimmer, with a surface temperature of 5500–11,000 °F (see Table 4). The temperature of a star depends on its mass, the more massive a star is, the hotter it gets.

The life of a star follows a definite pattern. Stars are borne in **nebulae**, clouds of hydrogen and helium gas and dust (see page 21). The clouds condense and star clusters form in the condensing gas, as the cores of the young stars reach a high enough temperature to trigger nuclear fusion reactions (see page 22). If the young star is massive it will form a white or blue star. If the young star is less massive it will be cooler and form a red, or

Table 4. Temperatures and Colors of Stars

Blue	20,000–45,000 °F	Rigel, Regulus
Blue-white	14,500–20,000 °F	Vega, Altair, Sirius
White	11,000–14,500 °F	Polaris, Procyon
Yellow-white	9000–11,000 °F	Sun, Capella
Orange	6500–9000 °F	Aldebaran, Arcturus
Red	5500–6500 °F	Betelgeuse, Antares

yellow star. Many more red and yellow stars are formed than white or blue ones.

Yellow dwarf stars like our Sun have long lifetimes, about 10,000 million years, during which time the hydrogen in their cores is gradually converted to helium. Eventually when all the hydrogen is used up and even the helium is converted to carbon, the Sun becomes unstable and expands, becoming much larger, cooler and more luminous. It has become a **red giant** like Aldebaran or Arcturus. Eventually the giant becomes so extended that its outer layers drift into space, forming a **planetary nebula** like the Ring Nebula in Lyra (see page 23). At the center of this planetary nebula remains a small **white dwarf star**, in which is condensed most of the mass of the star. White dwarfs do not generate energy by nuclear fusion and gradually radiate their remaining heat, cooling down in the process to become red dwarfs and eventually cold black dwarfs. The whole process takes thousands of millions of years.

Hotter, much more massive stars have much shorter, more spectacular lives. Stars such as Spica, which has a surface temperature of 43,000 °F, have a lifetime of about 100 million years. When their hydrogen and helium are all used up they expand to become **blue supergiants** like Rigel and then become **red supergiants** like Betelgeuse as they cool down. They may become very unstable and explode, forming a **supernova** instead of a planetary nebula. During the explosion they increase enormously in brightness and the outer layers of the star are thrown off into space. The remains of the supernova seen on Earth in 1054 is the Crab nebula (see page 24). At the same time as the explosion, the center of the star implodes, forming a condensed collapsed remnant known as a **neutron star**. A neutron star may measure only 12 miles across but contain the mass of one or two of our Suns. Neutron stars spin very rapidly and function as **pulsars**, sending out pulses of radio waves. The Crab Nebula pulsar pulses 30 times per second.

If the supergiant star is even more massive, then a mass equivalent to more than three of our Suns may remain in the condensed remnant after the supernova explosion. The enormous gravity of such a body is such that it prevents anything from leaving its surface, even light, and a **black hole** is formed. It is thought that at the centers of galaxies, where the matter was originally very dense, very massive stars were formed. These exploded very long ago, leaving black holes which have grown and coalesced so that now there are black holes at the centers of galaxies.

LIFE OF A STAR

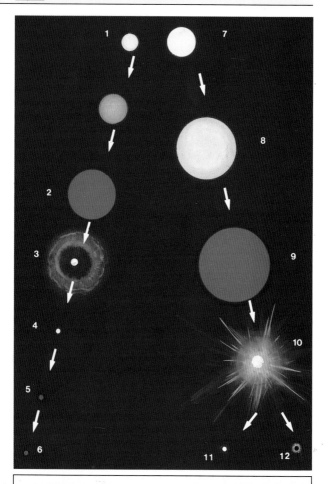

A. Yellow dwarf (1) → red giant (2) → planetary nebula (3) → white dwarf (4) → red dwarf (5) → black dwarf (6).
B. Blue star (7) → blue-white supergiant (8) → red supergiant (9) → supernova (10) → neutron star (11) or black hole (12).

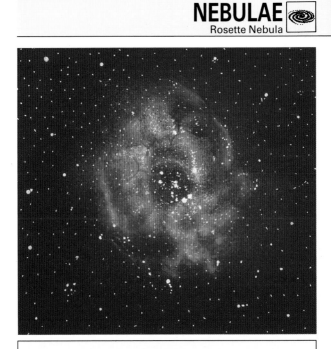

Nebulae are clouds of gas (mostly hydrogen) and dust, most common along the plane of the Milky Way. They do not shine with light of their own and can only be seen if lit by the light of stars, like the four stars of the Trapezium in the Orion Nebula. Dark nebulae, like the Horsehead Nebula in Orion and the Coalsack in the Southern Cross, can only be seen if they show up against a brighter background. The most easy nebula to see is the Orion Nebula (see page 53) but the Rosette Nebula in Monoceros and the Lagoon Nebula in Sagittarius are also visible in binoculars. New star clusters are born in nebulae like these, when the gas and dust clouds condense to form stars. In Hind's Variable Nebula in Taurus, T Tauri is a variable star thought to be so young that it is not yet stable; the T Tauri class of stars is named after it.

The Rosette Nebula is a complex system of gas and dust with a young cluster of about 16 stars being formed from it. It lies about 3600 light years away. The stars and the three brightest sections of the nebula are visible in amateur telescopes.

OPEN STAR CLUSTERS

The star clusters that are formed from the nebulae are known as open clusters. They are associations of young stars that move together in the general rotation around the galaxy. They are influenced by the other stars around them, so that the clusters gradually break up and drift apart. Our Sun was almost certainly formed in such a cluster about 4600 million years ago.

The most easy open clusters to see are the Pleiades and the Hyades, both in the constellation Taurus, and Praesepe the Beehive Cluster, in Cancer. The Pleiades contains about 250 stars, seven of which are visible to the naked eye. The stars are all close together and many are young, hot blue giant stars. The Hyades, which forms the face of the bull in Taurus, is an older, looser cluster in which the stars have drifted apart somewhat. The Beehive Cluster contains about 75 scattered stars about 520 light years away.

The Ring Nebula in Lyra is a planetary nebula. It appears to be an elliptical hazy disk in small telescopes, but can be seen to be shaped like a ring in large telescopes or on long-exposure photographs. Such a planetary nebula is formed when the outer layers of a red giant drift off into space. At the center of this nebula is a small white dwarf sun.

The Dumbbell Nebula is shaped like a figure of eight; it is found in Vulpecula, a small faint constellation near the head of Cygnus, the Swan. The largest planetary nebula visible from Earth is the Helix Nebula (NGC 7293) in Aquarius. It covers an area half the apparent size of the moon but is quite faint.

The Crab Nebula (M 1) in Taurus represents the remains of the supernova which was seen on Earth in 1054. In small telescopes it only appears to be a nebulous haze but in large telescopes its true form can be seen. There is a neutron star (a pulsar) at its center, the first to be detected by light as well as by radio pulses.

The Veil Nebula (NGC 6992) in Cygnus is another supernova remnant, which forms an even more tenuous nebula than the Crab Nebula.

Variable Stars

Several kinds of stars are known that, instead of shining constantly, vary in magnitude either periodically or irregularly. Some of them are truly variable stars; others, known as eclipsing variables, are actually double stars where one partner passes in front of the other and eclipses it for a period of time.

Cepheid Variables, named after Delta (δ) Cephei the first of its kind to be described, vary predictably in brightness because they vary in size. They pulsate regularly over a set period of time, usually between 2–40 days. Delta Cephei varies from mag. 3.6–4.3 every 5.4 days. Other stars that vary predictably include the blue giant **RR Lyrae** stars, common in globular clusters, which have periods of less than a day and which vary by about one magnitude.

Mira variables are old red giant or supergiant stars, named after Mira Ceti, the first to be discovered, which vary through several magnitudes over long periods of time. Mira Ceti varies from 3rd to 9th magnitude over a period of about 330 days. During this time it varies in diameter from 300 to 400 times that of our Sun.

Betelgeuse is a famous example of a **semi-regular variable**, a red supergiant with comparatively small, erratic changes in magnitude, from 0.4 to 1.3, changing from 300 to 400 times the diameter of our Sun at the same time.

Eruptive variable stars flare up from time to time, becoming very much more brilliant than previously, increasing by several magnitudes, for a period of days or months before fading again. **Novae** are stars of this kind; they are binary stars, large stars with white dwarf companions. The large star is expanding and periodically gases overflow onto the white dwarf, triggering a nuclear explosion. **Flare stars** are also eruptive variables; their increase in brilliance is thought to be due to a sudden increase in flare activity on their surface.

Double Stars

Many stars, although they appear single to the naked eye or even through a telescope, are actually double stars. They consist of two separate stars so close together that they cannot be separated visually but only by spectroscopic analysis — when it becomes obvious that two stars with different spectra are involved. The two stars are called **spectroscopic binaries**. In such a double star, one does not revolve around the other;

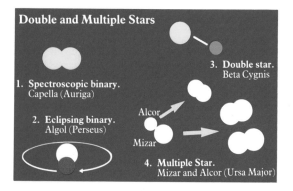

Double and Multiple Stars

1. **Spectroscopic binary.** Capella (Auriga)

2. **Eclipsing binary.** Algol (Perseus)

3. **Double star.** Beta Cygnis

Alcor

Mizar

4. **Multiple Star.** Mizar and Alcor (Ursa Major)

instead their common center of gravity lies somewhere between them and they both orbit around this.

Eclipsing binaries are a special kind of spectroscopic double stars. Algol (Beta Persei) is the prototype for this kind of star. Every 2 days 11 hours it decreases in magnitude from mag. 2 to 3.5 over a period of 5 hours, remains at minimum for 20 minutes, then takes 5 hours to reach maximum again. Algol consists of two stars; when the magnitude drops, its brighter blue-white star is eclipsed by the fainter yellow star.

Other double stars are further apart in space and can be seen either with the naked eye or with telescopes. Some, like Gamma Arietis and Beta Cygnis, are easy to separate; while others, like Delta Geminorum are much more difficult, requiring larger telescopes. Often the two stars are of different colors.

Some are **optical doubles** — they appear to be close to each other but in fact their closeness is an optical illusion — one is much further away than the other.

Multiple Stars

When examined closely some apparently double stars turn out to be multiple systems. One such is Mizar and Alcor, Zeta of Ursa Major. Mizar and Alcor form an optical double (they are 20 light years apart) which can be separated by binoculars. However Mizar actually forms a multiple system; it is a spectroscopic binary and has another fourth magnitude related companion which is also a spectroscopic binary. Alcor is yet another spectroscopic binary. Other multiple systems are Castor in Gemini and the Double Double in Lyra.

Finding the Stars

Because our Sun lies on the edge of one of the outer arms of the Milky Way, we are in an area of space where stars are not very numerous. If our Sun were in the central bulge of the Milky Way or in a globular cluster, there would be very many more stars visible to the naked eye. However it would be much more difficult (if not impossible) to observe the distant galaxies, because the light from the close stars would obscure our view.

Men have been star gazing since very early times and from the beginning they have attempted to make sense of the star patterns by making pictures in the sky. We know these patterns as **constellations**. There are 88 constellations in the sky. A constellation does not just include the stars of the pattern, but also the sky around it. The sky is thus divided into 88 separate sections. Many constellations are large and contain many interesting features, others are small and insignificant, covering small areas of the sky and containing few objects of interest. We have featured 38 constellations in this book. These include all the major northern constellations, together with some important or interesting ones which more properly belong to the southern hemisphere, but which can be seen low down in the southern horizon at certain times of year from 30° North, the latitude we have chosen as our southern limit.

The Earth rotates once every 24 hours and orbits the Sun once a year. Therefore which constellations are in view depends on time of night and time of year. During the day the Sun's light outshines the stars. As the Earth rotates into darkness the stars become visible, and the constellations change with the rotation. Those visible in the evening are not the same as those visible near dawn; the rotation of the Earth constantly brings new stars into view (they rise in the east) while others disappear (setting in the west). The constellations visible also depend on the latitude of the Earth from which they are viewed. If you stood at the north pole, your field of view would be restricted by the bulge of the Earth and you would only be able to see the northern constellations that appear to circle the pole, but they would be visible throughout the year. The same situation in reverse would be true of the South Pole. If you stood on the equator the rotation of the Earth would bring all the constellations into view during the course of a year, although the most northerly and most southerly ones would only just be visible above the horizon.

Between latitudes 30° North and 70° North (the zone into

which most of the USA and Canada falls), the constellations that can be seen represent a compromise between these two extremes. All the circumpolar constellations can be seen throughout the year and in the USA the more northerly of the southern constellations rotate into view during the year.

Locating the constellations

One of the easiest ways to find your way around the sky is to learn to recognize three or four key constellations or star patterns which serve as markers for all the others. We have used the Big Dipper and Orion (which most people know) together with Cassiopeia and the Summer Triangle (which are less familiar but easy to learn) as our markers and the other northern constellations can be located with reference to these four star patterns. The Summer Triangle is not a constellation but a triangle of three bright stars in three separate constellations which stand out clearly from the rest of the stars. Some of our featured constellations are too far south to be located from these key northern constellations. These can be seen in the southern sky at certain times of the year. Table 5 shows the key constellations, together with the featured constellations which can be found from them. These groupings are maintained in the constellation section.

Some of the constellations can be located from more than one key constellation, for instance Draco can be located from the Big Dipper or from the Summer Triangle. Others, although we have located them from northern key constellations, are quite far south and can be located by looking for them low in the southern sky. Eridanus and Hydra are such constellations. The positions of all the constellations relative to one another can be seen in the circular sky charts in the end papers of this book, and their seasonal positions in the sky are shown in the seasonal sky charts which follow.

On a really dark night the Milky Way will be seen stretching as a band across the sky. It acts as a good marker for the constellations of (from east to west) Monoceros, Gemini, Auriga, Perseus, Cassiopeia, Cygnus, Aquila, Sagittarius and Scorpius.

Using the Star Charts

The star charts which follow on the next eight pages illustrate the constellations which you can see in Spring, Summer, Fall and Winter, from the northern hemisphere. On the left hand pages are the constellations you will see facing north, on the right hand pages are those you will see facing south. Those on the left hand pages (the northern constellations) will change little, because they are the circumpolar constellations, those on the right hand pages will change from season to season as the Earth progresses around its orbit (see page 27). The horizon is represented by several separate curved lines, to allow for differences in latitude, from 10° North to 60° North.

All the constellations will change in position as the Earth rotates through the night. The positions of the constellations in the star charts are approximately those that will be seen between 10 pm and midnight (11 pm and midnight in daylight saving time). These positions will change by about 15° for each hour (the Earth rotates through 360° in 24 hours).

The Ecliptic

The ecliptic is the line followed by the Sun as it passes through the heavens in the course of a year. It passes through the signs of the zodiac in their astrological sequence and is marked in on the star charts as a dotted line. The planets also follow this path through the heavens and are best searched for along it. No patterns can be allocated to the planets as is done for the stars, for their positions change relative to the Earth from year to year.

Table 5. Key Constellations and their groups

Summer Triangle
Aquila
Cygnus
Lyra
Hercules
Ophiuchus
Serpens

Cassiopeia
Cepheus
Perseus
Andromeda
Pegasus
Aries
Pisces
Cetus

Orion
Auriga
Taurus
Eridanus
Lepus
Canis Major
Monoceros
Gemini
Cancer

The Big Dipper (Ursa Major)
Ursa Minor
Draco
Boötes and Corona Borealis
Virgo
Leo
Hydra

Southern constellations
Centaurus
Libra
Scorpius
Sagittarius
Capricornus
Aquarius

SPRING (April)
Facing north

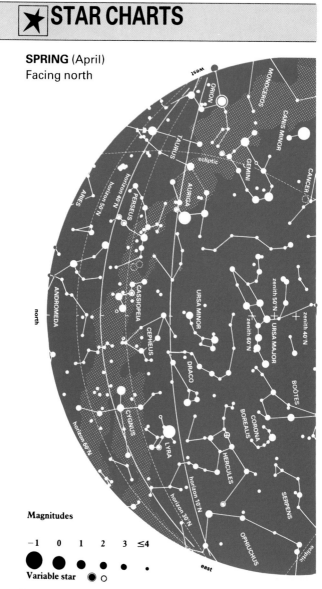

Magnitudes

−1 0 1 2 3 ≤4

Variable star ◉ ○

STAR CHARTS ★

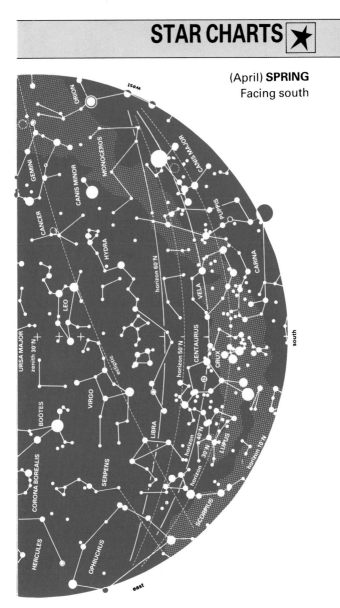

(April) **SPRING**
Facing south

SUMMER (July)
Facing north

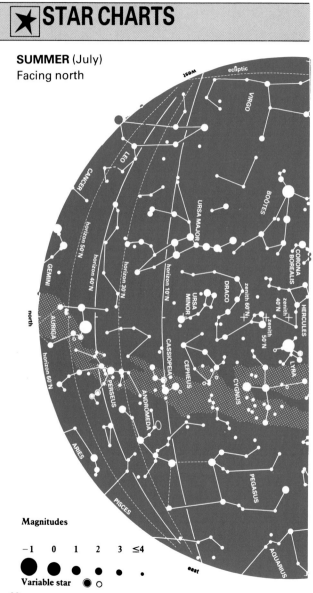

Magnitudes

−1   0   1   2   3   ≤4

Variable star ◉ ○

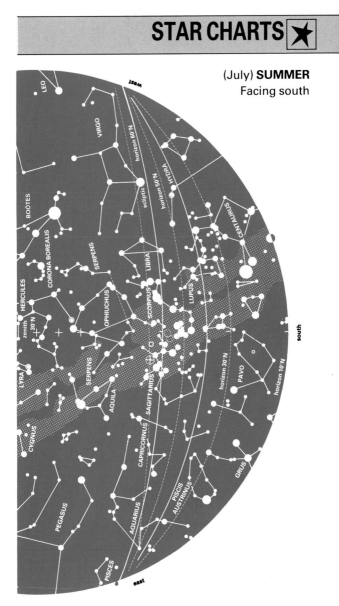

(July) **SUMMER**
Facing south

33

FALL (October)
Facing north

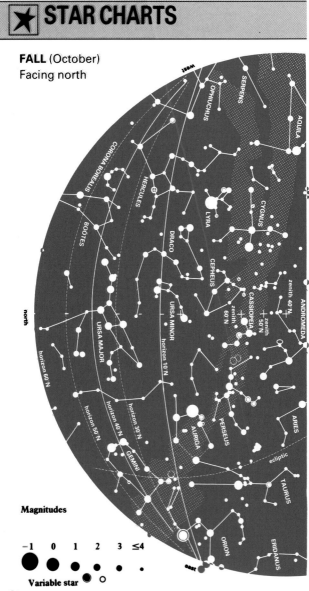

Magnitudes

-1 0 1 2 3 ≤4

Variable star ● ○

34

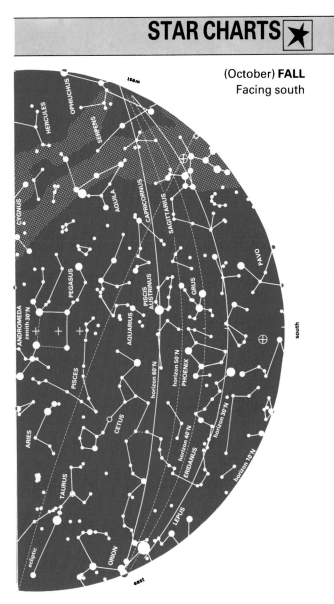

(October) **FALL**
Facing south

WINTER (January)
Facing north

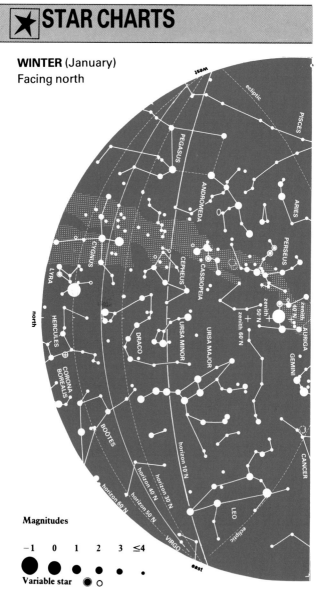

Magnitudes

−1 0 1 2 3 ≤4

Variable star

STAR CHARTS ★

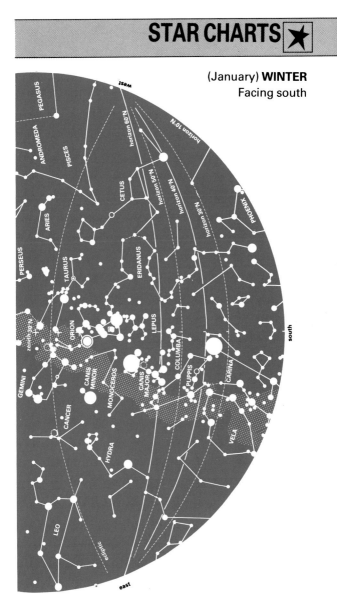

(January) **WINTER**
Facing south

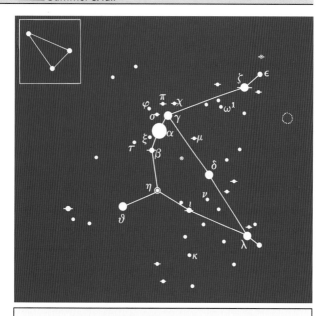

Altair, the brightest star in Aquila, is the most southerly star of the Summer Triangle, lying just on the edge of the Milky Way. The other stars of the triangle are Vega (in Lyra) and Deneb (in Cygnus).

Altair is one of the closest stars to the Sun and the 12th brightest star in the sky. It is readily identifiable as the central and brightest star in a line of three, with **Gamma** (γ) and **Delta** (δ), both yellow stars, on either side. **Eta** (η) is a bright Cepheid variable, varying every seven days.

Towards the west Aquila contains rich star fields where it overlaps the Milky Way. In this region the Milky Way is obscured by dark clouds of dust, which look like a great rift extending from Scutum past Aquila towards Cygnus.

α (Altair) white, mag. 0.77, 16 l.y.: γ (Tarazed) yellow giant, mag. 2.7, 284 l.y.: ζ blue-white, mag. 3, 104 l.y.: θ blue-white, mag. 3.2, 200 l.y.. δ white, mag. 3.4, 52 l.y.: λ blue-white, mag. 3.4, 98 l.y.: β (Alshain) yellow, mag. 3.7, 42 l.y.: η Cepheid variable, mag. 4–5.3, 1400 l.y.

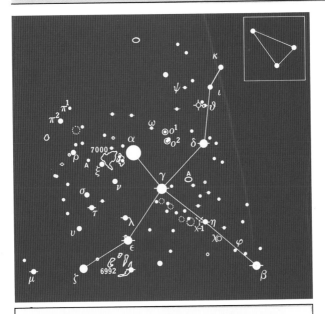

A swan with wings outstretched, flying along the Milky Way. Also called the Northern Cross. **Deneb**, the brightest of its stars, is the most northerly star of the Summer Triangle.

There are several good doubles in Cygnus, including **Beta** (β) with a yellow giant and blue-green companion, **Omicron** (o) a pair of orange and turquoise stars, **Mu** (μ) a fainter pair of white dwarfs, and **Psi** (ψ) a pair of white stars.

The Milky Way in this area is obscured by the dark clouds of the **Northern Coalsack**. The many bright nebulae include **NGC 7000**, a cloud of gas known as the **North America Nebula**. The **Veil Nebula** (**NGC 6992**) is the remnant of a supernova.

Cygnus X–1 is probably a black hole, it is a source of X-rays. **Cygnus A** is a source of radio waves and is believed to be two distant galaxies in collision.

α (Deneb) blue-white supergiant, mag. 1.25, 1800 l.y.: γ yellow supergiant, mag. 2.2, 750 l.y.: β (Albireo) double, mag. 3.1, 390 l.y.: ϵ yellow giant, mag. 2.5, 82 l.y.: δ blue-white with close companion, mag. 2.9, 160 l.y.

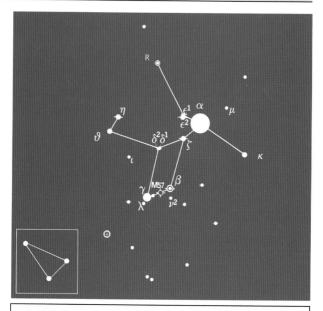

A small but easily recognized constellation close to the Milky Way. It represents a lyre, an ancient stringed instrument. **Vega**, the brightest star in Lyra is also the brightest star in the Summer Triangle, and fifth brightest in the sky.

Sheliak is a multiple star with one yellow and one blue star. The brighter yellow star is an eclipsing binary that varies from mag. 3.5 to 4.3 every 12.9 days. The stars are so close they are distorted by gravity. The **Double Double** is a famous quadruple star, with two double stars oriented almost at right angles to each other, a rare combination. They can be seen in 75 mm telescopes.

The **Ring Nebula**, **M 57**, is one of the brightest planetary nebulae, appearing as an elliptical hazy disk in small telescopes.

α (Vega) blue-white, mag. 0.03, 26 l.y.: γ blue-white, mag. 3.2, 190 l.y.: β (Sheliak) double, mag. 3.4 max, 300 l.y.: ϵ (The Double Double), mag. 3.9, 120 l.y.: ζ double, mag. 4.4, 210 l.y.: η blue-white with wide companion, mag. 4.4, 880 l.y.

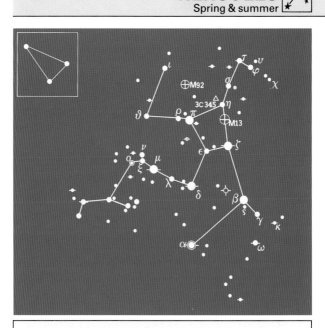

The **Keystone**, an irregular rectangle of four stars forms the center of Hercules. It lies close to Lyra, on a line drawn between Vega in Lyra and Arcturus in Boötes.

There are many double stars in Hercules, including **Gamma** (γ), **Zeta** (ζ), **Kappa** (κ) and **Rho** (ρ). **Ras Algethi** (α) is one of the largest stars known, with a diameter 600 times greater than that of the Sun; its size makes it erratically variable. It has a blue-green companion visible in small telescopes.

One of the brightest globular clusters visible from the northern hemisphere, **M 13** (see also page 17), lies between **Eta** (η) and **Zeta** (ζ) on the Keystone. It is about 22,500 light years away, measures over 100 light years in diameter and contains about 300,000 stars; individual stars are visible through a small telescope. **M 92**, a cluster 36,000 light years away, is denser than M 13 and individual stars are more difficult to see.

α (Ras Algethi) red supergiant, mag. 3–4, 540 l.y.: β yellow giant, mag. 2.8, 100 l.y.: γ white, mag. 3.8, 140 l.y.: ζ yellow, mag. 2.8, 31 l.y.: π orange, mag. 3.2, 390 l.y.

41

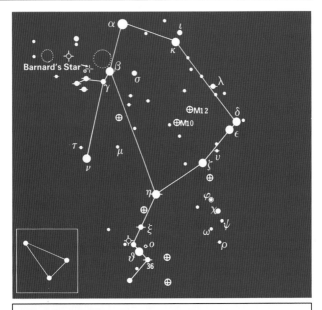

The club of Hercules points towards the head of Ophiuchus. The constellation represents a man encircled by a Serpent. Only part can be seen from the northern hemisphere.

The 9th magnitude red dwarf, **Barnard's Star**, is the 2nd closest star to the Sun and appears to move more rapidly than any other star, relative to Earth, covering a distance equivalent to the apparent diameter of the Moon in 180 years. There are several double and multiple stars in Ophiuchus, including **Rho** (ρ), a multiple with a close double and two wide companions; and **36 Ophiuchus**, a pair of orange dwarfs.

Ophiuchus extends into the Milky Way and contains many globular clusters. Two of the finest, **M 10** and **M 12**, can both be seen with binoculars or a small telescope.

α (Ras Alhague) white, mag. 2.1, 62 l.y.: β yellow giant, mag. 2.8, 120 l.y.: γ blue-white, mag. 3.8, 115 l.y.: δ orange giant, mag. 2.7, 140 l.y.: ϵ orange giant, mag. 3.2, 105 l.y.: ζ blue-white, mag. 2.6, 550 l.y.: η blue-white, mag. 2.4, 59 l.y.: θ blue-white, mag. 3.3, 590 l.y.

This constellation represents a serpent encircling Ophiuchus, the Serpent Holder and is split into two halves, one on each side of Ophiuchus. Its head lies between Ophiuchus and Arcturus in Boötes; its fainter tail runs alongside the Milky Way and up into the long dark clouds that obscure the Milky Way at this point.

The Serpent's head is made up of a triangle of three stars. In this area lies **M 5**, one of the finest globular clusters in the northern sky, considered second only to M 13 in Hercules. In a 100 mm telescope the cluster can be seen to have a dense center with chains of stars radiating outwards in its outer zones. It is 27,000 light years away and may just be visible to the naked eye in good conditions.

M 16 is a nebulous star cluster, enveloped in a hazy cloud of dust. It is 8000 light years away and visible, with binoculars, in the Serpent's tail just inside the Milky Way.

α orange giant, mag. 2.7, 85 l.y.: β blue-white, mag. 3.7, 120 l.y.: γ white, mag. 3.9, 39 l.y.: η orange, mag. 3.3, 52 l.y.: θ double white, mag. 3.4, 100 l.y.

43

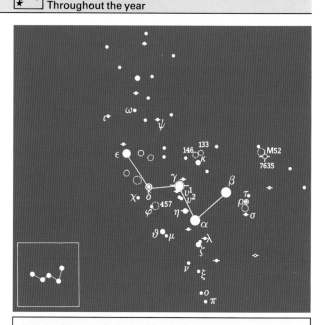

A distinctive constellation and one of the most easy to recognize, its W shape lying along the Milky Way.

Gamma (γ) is a shell star, rotating so rapidly that it throws off rings of gas at irregular intervals. There are several double stars in Cassiopeia, including **Eta** (η), a yellow and red pair and **Sigma** (σ), a green and blue pair. **Iota** (ι) is a triple star, a white primary with two companions.

Cassiopeia has rich clouds of dust and nebulae and many star clusters. **NGC 457** is a bright open cluster close to **Phi** (φ) which is a yellow supergiant star, mag. 5. Both star and cluster are clearly visible with small telescopes. Open clusters **NGC 133** and **146** are found northeast of **Beta** (β) near to **Kappa** (κ). The **Bubble Nebula, NGC 7635**, a cloud of gas like the top of a bubble, is close to another rich cluster, **M 52**.

α (Shedar) yellow giant with wide faint companion, mag. 2.2, 120 l.y.: β (Caph) white, mag. 2.3, 42 l.y.: γ blue giant variable, mag. 1.6–3, 780 l.y.: δ (Ruchbah) blue-white, mag. 2.7, 62 l.y.: ε blue giant, mag. 3.4, 520 l.y.

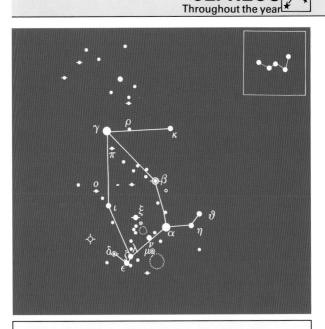

A line through Alpha and Beta of Cassiopeia points towards Cepheus. There are several famous stars in Cepheus, including **Delta** (δ) which is the prototype for the whole class of stars known as Cepheid variables (see page 25). It varies from its faintest to its brightest in 5 days 9 hrs, its change being visible from one night to the next. It is also a double star with a faint wide blue companion.

Mu (μ) is known as the **Garnet Star**, from its deep red color which can be seen with the naked eye. It is the prototype for the class of stars known as semi-regular variables.

Beta (β) is another variable star, but its variation can only be detected by instruments. Beta is a double star, with a blue giant primary and a fainter, 8th magnitude companion.

α (Alderamin) white, mag. 2.4, 46 l.y.: β (Alphirk) double and variable, mag. 3.2, 750 l.y.: γ yellow, mag. 3.2, 52 l.y.: δ yellow giant variable, mag. 3.6–4.3, 1300 l.y.: μ red supergiant variable, mag. 3.6–5.1, 1600 l.y.

45

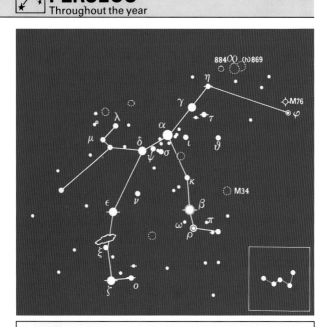

A complex constellation lying along the Milky Way east of Cassiopeia. The famous red double star, **Algol** (also known as the Winking Demon), is the prototype for the eclipsing binary type of star. The two partners orbit around each other in such a way that the dimmer one periodically eclipses the brighter member (see also page 26).

The famous **Double Cluster** (**NGC 869** and **884**), sometimes called h and χ (chi) Persei, is easily visible through binoculars, when they can be viewed simultaneously. The former is the richer and brighter with 350 stars, the latter has about 300. They both lie about 7000 light years away. Other clusters in Perseus include **M 76** and **M 34**.

α (Algenib) yellow supergiant, mag. 1.8, 620 l.y.: β (Algol) eclipsing binary, mag. 2.2–3.5, 95 l.y.: γ yellow giant, mag. 2.9, 110 l.y.: ε blue-white, mag. 2.9, 680 l.y.: ζ blue supergiant, mag. 2.9, 1100 l.y.: δ blue giant, mag. 3, 330 l.y.: η double, mag. 3.8, 820 l.y.: ρ variable red giant, mag. 3.3–4.0, 200 l.y.

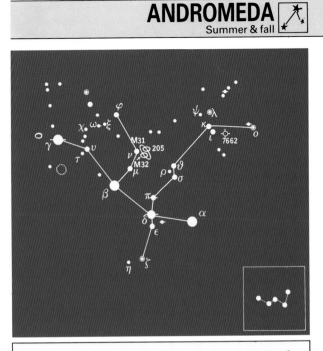

The four stars that form the line of the body and the right leg of the constellation are the most obvious. They run in a crooked line parallel to the Milky Way alongside Cassiopeia, with **Alpheratz** forming one corner of the square of Pegasus and the other end pointing at Perseus.

The triple star, **Gamma** (γ) consists of a bright yellow star with a double pair of blue stars as a companion.

The **Andromeda Galaxy** (**M 31**), is 2.2. million light years away, the closest spiral galaxy to.our own and the only one visible to the naked eye (see also page 16).

NGC 7662 is one of the best planetary nebulae for small telescopes or binoculars, appearing as a blue-green hazy disk, showing its ring-like appearance at higher powers in the telescope.

α (Alpheratz) blue-white, mag. 2.1, 105 l.y.: β (Mirach), red giant, mag. 2.1, 88 l.y.: γ triple, mag. 2.1, 120 l.y.: δ orange giant, mag. 3.3, 160 l.y.

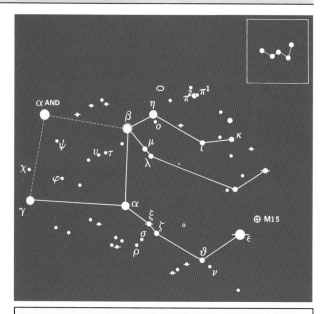

This large constellation resembles the body, head and fore legs of a horse. Its most noticeable feature is the **Square of Pegasus** (the body of the horse), a huge square of four stars with very few other naked eye stars in the area. The fourth star of this square, at one time Delta (δ) Pegasi, is now part of Andromeda. The constellation lies to the east of the Milky Way, with the W-shape of Cassiopeia pointing towards it.

M 15 is one of the brightest globular clusters in the sky, although it is 50,000 light years away. It appears as a hazy patch with the naked eye; in binoculars its multiple nature becomes apparent, with a condensed center and diffuse edges. The stars themselves can be differentiated with larger telescopes.

α (Markab) blue-white, mag. 2.5, 100 l.y.: β red giant variable, 2.4 max., 180 l.y.: γ blue-white, mag. 2.8, 490 l.y.: ε (Enif) yellow supergiant, mag. 2.4, 520 l.y.: η yellow giant, mag. 2.9, 170 l.y.: ζ white, mag. 3.4, 160 l.y.

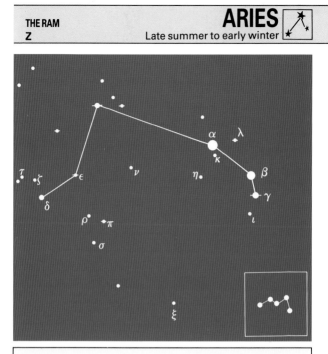

A small constellation which lies south of the line of stars marking Andromeda. The group of three stars, **Alpha** (α), **Beta** (β), and **Gamma** (γ) are the most easily recognizable. The constellation is said to represent the Golden Fleece sought by Jason and the Argonauts.

There are several double stars in Aries. Two of them are easily divisible in small telescopes, **Mesarthim** (γ) and **Lambda** (λ), a white star of magnitude 4.8 which has a yellow, 7th magnitude companion. Doubles which need larger telescopes to separate them are **Epsilon** (ϵ), a close pair of white stars, magnitudes 5.3 and 5.6; and **Pi** (π), a white star with a faint close companion.

α (Hamal) yellow giant, mag. 2, 85 l.y.: β (Sheratan) white, mag. 2.6, 46 l.y.: γ (Mesarthim) double white, mag. 3.9, 160 l.y.

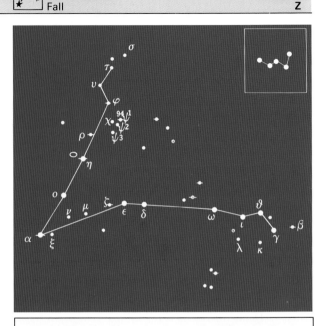

The constellation is supposed to represent two fishes tied together by their tails at **Alpha** (α). It is rather faint, with its brightest star, **Eta** (η), having a magnitude of 3.6. It lies south of Pegasus, with Alpha (α), sometimes called the knot, pointing towards Cetus. The stars **Iota** (ι), **Theta** (θ), **Gamma** (γ), **Kappa** (κ) and **Lambda** (λ) form a pentagon south of the square of Pegasus, sometimes called the Circlet.

Alpha (α) is a double star whose components are quite difficult to separate in small telescopes since they are close together. **Zeta** (ζ) is a much easier double, both stars are visible even in very small telescopes. **Rho** (ρ) forms an optical double with a quite unrelated, giant orange star, **94 Piscium**. **Psi** (ψ) is a wide double star with two blue-white stars visible in binoculars or a small telescope. They have magnitudes of 5.3 and 5.6.

α blue-white double, mag. 4.3, 98 l.y.: δ yellow giant, mag. 3.7, 160 l.y.: η yellow giant, mag. 3.6, 140 l.y.: ρ white, mag. 5.4, 98 l.y.: ζ double, mag. 4.9, 110 l.y.

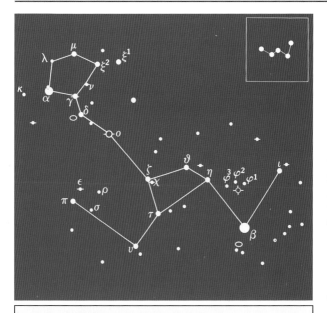

A large constellation best seen facing south on fall evenings. The knot of Pisces points towards **Mira** (*o*) in Cetus.

Mira is a famous star, prototype of the Mira class of long-period variables and the first variable star to be discovered (see page 25).

Tau Ceti (*τ*) is one of the closest stars to the Sun. It is very similar in size and spectrum to our Sun and has been investigated for planets and signs of life, with no result so far. **UV Ceti** is also close to the Sun. It is a red dwarf and a flare star, brightening unpredictably for a few minutes, from its normal 13th magnitude to 7th magnitude.

M 77 is a spiral galaxy and a radio source. It is too far and faint, 50 million light years away and 9th magnitude, to be more than a glowing patch in small telescopes.

α red giant, mag. 2.5, 130 l.y.: *β* yellow giant, mag. 2, 68 l.y.: *γ* double, mag. 3.5, 75 l.y.: *τ* yellow dwarf, mag. 3.5, 11.7 l.y.: *η* orange giant, mag. 3.5, 120 l.y.: *o* (Mira) red giant variable, 820 l.y.

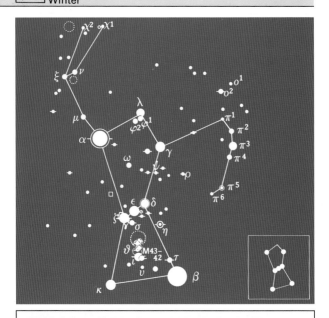

One of the most easily recognized constellations in the sky, hanging in the southern sky on winter nights. The Hunter is brandishing a club (a lopsided Y of five stars) and shield (a curving line of five stars) at Taurus. From his bright belt of three stars hangs his sword (the **Orion Nebula**).

The three stars of Orion's Belt are **Alnitak**, a blue-white star, **Alnilam** (the string of pearls) a blue-white supergiant and **Mintaka**, a double star of a blue-white giant and a fainter companion. Just below Alnitak is a bright hazy area with a dark cloud of dust in front of it, the **Horsehead Nebula**, visible only on long exposure photographs.

α (Betelgeuse) red supergiant, mag. 0.4–1.3, 310 l.y.: β (Rigel) blue-white supergiant, mag. 0.1, 900 l.y.: γ (Bellatrix) blue giant, mag. 1.6, 360 l.y.: ϵ (Alnilam) blue supergiant, mag. 1.7, 1200 l.y.: ζ (Alnitak) blue-white, mag. 1.8, 1100 l.y.: δ (Mintaka) blue-white double, mag. 2.2, 2350 l.y.: χ (Saiph) blue supergiant, mag. 2.1, 2100 l.y.: λ blue-white, mag. 3.7, 1400 l.y.: σ blue-white, mag. 3.7, 1800 l.y.

Betelgeuse (α) is a red supergiant, a huge unstable sun which fluctuates irregularly in size and magnitude. **Rigel** (β), seventh brightest star in the sky, is a double star with a blue-white supergiant and a 7th magnitude companion, lost in the light from the primary in small telescopes. Other doubles where the companion is close to the primary and difficult to see are **Zeta** (ζ), **Eta** (η), **Lambda** (λ) and **Rho** (ρ). **Delta** (δ) is an eclipsing binary with a wide companion; **Iota** (ι) is a double star and **Sigma** (σ) has three companions, one of which can be seen in binoculars. In the same field of view as Sigma is **Struve 761**, a triangle of 8th and 9th magnitude stars.

Orion's sword hangs from his belt. It consists of the Orion nebula (see also page 21), swirls of gas and dust, the precursor of a star cluster. The lower swirl, **M 43**, is illuminated by **Theta** (θ), a single blue-white star to the naked eye but actually a group of four stars known as the **Trapezium**. The two gas swirls, **M 42** and **M 43** are part of the same cloud and only appear to be separated; they are greenish to the naked eye but appear red and blue in color photographs.

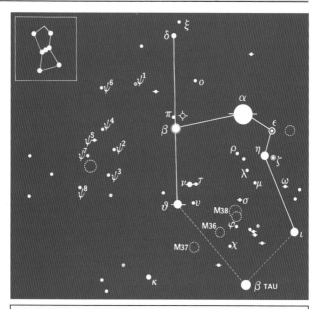

The club of Orion points towards Auriga, which straddles the Milky Way above the horns of Taurus. It is a large kite-shaped constellation with **Capella** as the left shoulder of a charioteer holding two small goat kids, the triangle of **Epsilon** (ϵ), **Eta** (η) and **Zeta** (ζ), in his left arm.

Capella is the sixth brightest star in the sky. Epsilon (ϵ) has a dark companion which orbits and eclipses it every 27 years; the eclipse lasts for about a year during which time the magnitude drops to 3.8.

Auriga is rich in features within the Milky Way. Several open clusters are visible with binoculars or a telescope. **M 37** is the richest with about 150 stars, **M 38** has about 100 scattered stars and **M 36** has about 60 bright stars.

α (Capella) yellow binary, mag. 0.08, 42 l.y.: β (Menkarlinan), blue-white eclipsing variable, mag. approx. 2, 72 l.y.: θ blue-white, mag. 2.6, 85 l.y.: ι orange, mag. 2.7, 267 l.y.: ϵ white supergiant eclipsing binary, mag. 3–3.8, 2000 l.y.: η blue-white, mag. 3.2, 199 l.y.

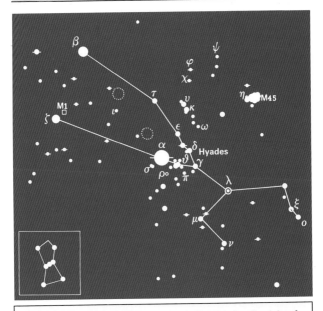

Visible on winter nights, high in the sky above and to the right of Orion with the shield of Orion between Taurus and the figure of the Hunter. The constellation represents the head of a bull with the Hyades forming its face.

The **Hyades** is a large open V-shaped cluster of about 200 stars, 150 light years away and best viewed with binoculars. **Aldebaran**, a giant red-orange star, which forms the eye of the Bull, appears to be part of the Hyades but is in fact much closer. The bull's horns are formed by **Beta** (β) and **Zeta** (ζ). Near the lower horn and visible as a faint wispy patch in small telescopes, is the **Crab Nebula, M 1** (see page 24).

The **Pleiades, M 45** (see also page 22) is a close cluster of 250 stars, 450 light years away. It is usually called the Seven Sisters since seven stars are visible to the naked eye. The brightest is **Alcyone**, mag. 2.9; **Pleione** is a shell star which throws off rings of gas at irregular intervals.

α (Aldebaran), red giant, mag. 0.9, 68 l.y.: β (El Nath), blue giant, mag. 1.7, 140 l.y.: ζ blue-white, mag. 3, 490 l.y.

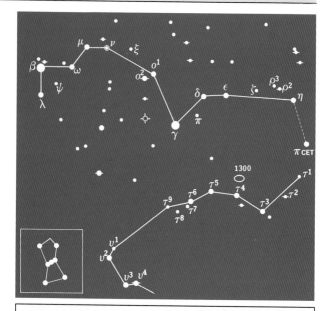

A long faint winding constellation that begins just beneath Rigel, the right foot of Orion, winds west beneath Taurus and then turns south to plunge deep in the southern hemisphere to end in the bright, first magnitude star of **Achernar**, near Phoenix. Only the part visible in the northern hemisphere is illustrated.

Epsilon (ϵ) is a star very like our own Sun and is believed to have a large planet or small star companion. **Omicron** (o) is a triple star, with a yellow dwarf and a white dwarf companion which itself has a red dwarf companion. This white dwarf is the closest white dwarf sun to the Sun and the easiest to observe in small telescopes.

NGC 1300 is a barred spiral galaxy, one of a cluster of galaxies in the constellation. Others are scattered throughout this region of space.

β (Cursa), blue-white, mag. 2.8, 85 l.y.: γ orange giant, mag. 2.9, 140 l.y.: ϵ yellow dwarf, mag. 3.7, 10.7 l.y.: o triple, mag. 4.4, 15.9 l.y.

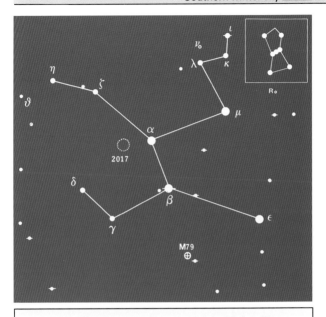

A small constellation that lies beneath the feet of Orion. The two stars in **Gamma** (γ) are an orange-giant and a yellow companion, divisible in small telescopes, with magnitudes of 3.6 and 6.2 respectively. **R Leporis** is a red star which varies from 6th to 10th magnitude every 430 days.

M 79 is a rich globular cluster, one of the few visible in winter; it is 8th magnitude, 43,000 light years away and looks like a fuzzy star in small telescopes.

NGC 2017 is a small cluster of what looks like five stars, of from 7th to 10th magnitude, in small telescopes. In fact two of the stars are doubles so that seven stars are involved.

α yellow-white supergiant, mag. 2.6, 950 l.y.: β yellow giant, mag. 2.8, 320 l.y.: γ double, mag. 3.6, 27 l.y.: ϵ orange giant, mag. 3.2, 160 l.y.: μ blue-white, mag. 3.3, 215 l.y.

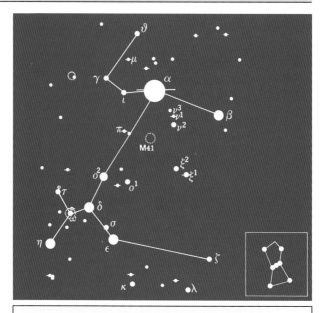

One of two dogs which follow at the heels of Orion, the Hunter. The belt of Orion points towards **Sirius**, the brightest star in the sky and one of the closest stars to our Sun. There is a fine open cluster of about 50 stars, **M 41**, just below Sirius; about 25 of these are visible through a small telescope. The cluster is about 2500 light years away.

α (Sirius), white, mag. −1.46, 8.6 l.y.: β pulsating blue giant, mag. 2, 710 l.y.: δ yellow supergiant, mag. 1.9, 3060 l.y.: ϵ blue giant, mag. 1.5, 490 l.y.: η blue supergiant, mag. 2.4, 2500 l.y.: ζ blue-white, mag. 3, 287 l.y.

Canis Minor, The Lesser Dog, is a small constellation above and to the left of Canis Major, on the opposite side of the Milky Way. Also known as the Lone Star Constellation, its "lone star" is **Procyon**, eighth brightest star in the sky. It is a yellow-white star, 11.3 light years away, magnitude 0.38.

The three stars, Procyon, Sirius and Betelgeuse (in Orion) form a prominent triangle of bright stars.

MONOCEROS
Winter & spring

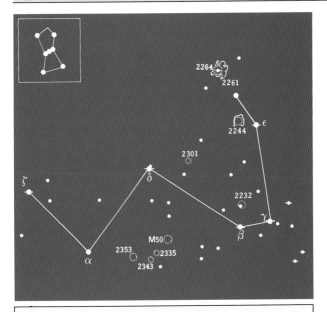

A faint constellation straddling the Milky Way beside Orion. **Beta** (β) is a fine triple star, consisting of an arc of three blue-white stars, visible through a small telescope.

The **Rosette Nebula** is a cloud of gas around the star cluster **NGC 2244**. Through small telescopes only the cluster and fragments of the nebula can be seen, but long exposure photographs show the nebula as a spectacular rosy ring (see also page 21). The **Cone Nebula**, **NGC 2264**, is another star cluster and nebula that is similarly difficult to view in small telescopes. **Hubble's Variable Nebula**, **NGC 2261**, is shaped like a comet's tail; it contains **R Monocerotis**, a variable star which fluctuates from 10th to 13th magnitude.

Other star clusters include **NGC 2301, 2335, 2343, 2232** and **M 50**, the two latter both visible in binoculars.

α orange giant, mag. 3.9, 180 l.y.: β triple, mag. 4.4, 720 l.y.: δ blue-white, mag. 4.2, 210 l.y.: ϵ double yellow and blue, mag. 4.3, 180 l.y.: γ orange giant, mag. 4, 200 l.y.: ζ yellow supergiant, mag. 4.3, 1800 l.y.

59

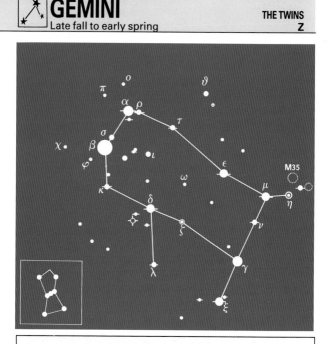

The arm of Orion points upwards and towards Gemini, which lies on the opposite side of the Milky Way. Gemini is a roughly rectangular constellation. The Twins are **Castor** and **Pollux**, the two brightest stars in the constellation. Castor appears to be a blue-white star; in fact it is a multiple system; two bright stars revolve around each other and they also have a fainter companion. Since each of the three is a double star, actually six stars are involved.

There are several variable stars in Gemini. **Zeta** (ζ) is a Cepheid variable, fluctuating every 10 days from magnitude 3.7 to 4.1. **Eta** (η) fluctuates in brightness every 230 days.

Near Eta is **M 35**, a large bright star cluster of about 120 stars, 1200 light years away. The stars lie in curving chains visible through a small telescope.

α (Castor) multiple, mag. 1.6, 36 l.y.: β (Pollux) orange giant, mag. 1.1, 46 l.y.: γ blue-white, mag. 1.9, 85 l.y.: ϵ yellow supergiant, mag. 3, 680 l.y.: μ red, 2.9, 230 l.y.: η red giant, mag. 3.1–3.9, 186 l.y.: ξ white, mag. 3.4, 75 l.y.

Cancer lies in the center of a rough triangle formed by Procyon in Canis Minor, Castor and Pollux in Gemini and Regulus in Leo. It is the faintest of the zodiac constellations, an inverted Y-shape with four major stars, only two of which are as bright as third magnitude.

Zeta (ζ) is a multiple star. It has two yellow stars of magnitudes 5.1 and 6, together with a fainter 6th magnitude companion, close to the brighter of the two.

Just to the right of **Gamma** (γ) and **Delta** (δ), more or less in the center of the constellation is **Praesepe the Manger**, or **Beehive Cluster** (**M 44**). It is a cluster of 75 stars, many of which are multiples, lying 520 light years away. It is best seen in binoculars. Gamma and Delta are sometimes called the Donkeys, supposedly because they are feeding at the Manger.

α (Acubens) white, mag. 4.3, 100 l.y.: β orange giant, mag. 3.5, 170 l.y.: γ white, mag. 4.7, 230 l.y.: ι yellow giant with fainter blue-white companion, mag. 4, 420 l.y.: δ yellow giant, mag. 3.9, 220 l.y.

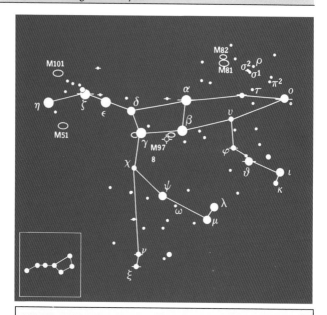

The best known star pattern in the sky, the Big Dipper, seven stars in the shape of a dipper, is part of this constellation. In Europe it is known as the Plough or the Wain (Wagon). Five of the seven stars are travelling together in space, but two of them, **Alkaid** and **Dubhe**, are moving in different directions.

The Dipper is part of a larger constellation which ancient peoples, including the Greeks and the American'Red Indians, recognized as a great bear. Its immediate recognizability makes the Dipper an important marker constellation. The curve of its handle points towards Arcturus in Boötes; a line through Merak and Dubhe points towards the North Star in Ursa Minor; while in the other direction a line through Dubhe from Merak points towards Leo.

α (Dubhe), yellow giant, mag. 1.8, 75 l.y.: β (Merak), white, mag. 2.4, 62 l.y.: γ (Phecda). white, mag. 75 l.y.: δ (Megrez), white, mag. 3.3, 65 l.y.: ϵ (Alioth), white, mag. 1.7, 78 l.y.: ζ (Mizar and Alcor), multiple, mag. 2.1, 60 l.y.: η (Alkaid), blue-white, mag. 1.9, 160 l.y.

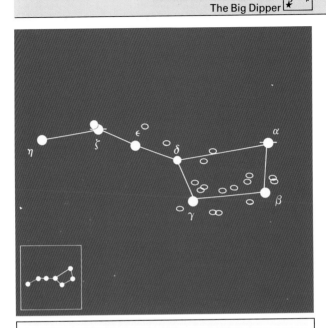

There are many galaxies in Ursa Major, many of them concentrated in the cup of the Dipper and extending diagonally downwards to the left. Another smaller group is located above and between Alkaid and Mizar. These galaxies are mostly very far away and faint so that only a few are visible in small telescopes.

However **M 81** and **M 101** are both famous galaxies and two of the brightest in the sky. M 81 is an 8th magnitude spiral galaxy visible as a roundish patch in small telescopes. Near to it is a 9th magnitude galaxy, **M 82**, edge on to us in a cloud of gas. Both are about 18 million light years away. M 101 is face on with spiral arms, and shows up as a glowing patch about half the apparent size of the full moon, in a small telescope. **M 51**, the **Whirlpool Galaxy**, is face on to us and shows the full beauty of its spiral form in large telescopes. It is 14 million light years away.

The **Owl Nebula**, **M 97**, is a cloud of gas and dust with two dark patches in it that look like eyes. It is 2600 light years away.

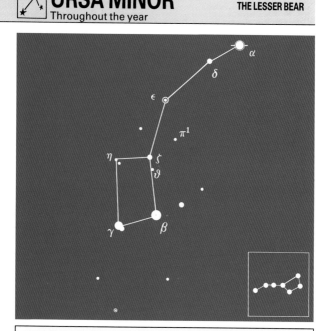

Also known as the Little Dipper, this constellation looks like a smaller edition of the Big Dipper with its handle ending in **Polaris**, the North Star. A line drawn through Merak and Dubhe in the Big Dipper points towards Polaris. The stars **Beta** (β) and **Gamma** (γ) are sometimes called the Guardians of the Pole or the Guards. Polaris is a Cepheid variable but varies very slightly; it is a double star with a 9th magnitude companion.

Polaris is very close to the celestial north pole (within 1°). It circles the pole once every 24 hours. Polaris is used in navigation to find north and can also be used to calculate the latitude of the point on Earth from which it is viewed. The altitude of Polaris is approximately equal to the latitude.

α (Polaris), yellow supergiant, mag. 2.1, 700 l.y.: β orange giant, mag. 2.1, 95 l.y.: γ blue-white, mag. 3.1, 230 l.y.: ζ blue-white, mag. 4.3, 110 l.y.: η white, mag. 5, 911 l.y.: δ blue-white, mag. 4.4, 140 l.y.: ϵ yellow giant with eclipsing companion, mag. 4.2, 200 l.y.

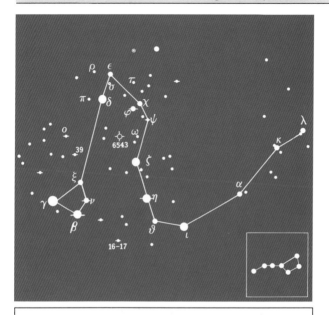

A long, relatively faint constellation which winds around Ursa Minor and separates the Little Dipper from the Big Dipper. The head of the Dragon forms a lozenge of four stars, near the base of the Summer Triangle. Two of the four are easily visible to the naked eye, the other two are fainter.

There are several multiple star systems within Draco including **Nu** (ν), a fine pair of white stars; **Psi** (ψ), a pair of yellow stars; **16–17**, a pair of blue-white stars, one of which has a companion; and **39**, with a blue star and a yellow star with a companion. All can be seen in binoculars but differentiation of the companions in the two latter systems needs a 60 mm telescope.

NGC 6543 is a planetary nebula, visible as a blue-green disk in telescopes. It is 1700 light years away.

α (Thuban) white, mag. 3.7, 230 l.y.: β yellow supergiant, mag. 2.8, 270 l.y.: γ (Eltanin) orange giant, mag. 2.2, 100 l.y.: ξ orange giant, mag. 3.2, 320 l.y.: ν white double, mag. 4.9, 120 l.y.

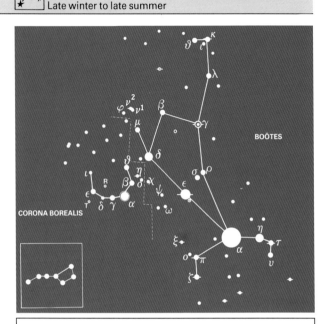

The handle of the Big Dipper points towards **Arcturus** in Boötes, The Herdsman. Arcturus, the third brightest star in the sky, forms the shape of a Y with **Epsilon** (ϵ) and **Gamma** (γ), together with **Gemma** (α) of Corona Borealis. Corona is a crown of seven stars, all but Gemma of the fourth magnitude.

In Boötes, Epsilon (ϵ) is a famous double star with an orange giant primary and a blue companion. **Mu** (μ) is a triple star, with a blue-white star orbited by a double companion.

Within the arc of Corona lies **R CrB**, a 6th magnitude star which fades every few years to 11th magnitude or fainter. The last drop occurred in 1962. **T CrB**, The Blaze Star, which lies outside the Crown, is a recurrent nova, brightening unpredictably to 2nd magnitude. Its last flare up was in 1946.

Boötes. α (Arcturus) red giant, mag. –0.04, 36 l.y.: β yellow giant, mag. 3.5, 140 l.y.: ϵ double, mag. 2.4, 150 l.y.: δ yellow giant, mag. 3.5, 140 l.y.: γ white, mag. 3, 105 l.y.
Corona Borealis. α (Gemma) blue-white, mag. 2.2, 78 l.y.: β white, mag. 3.7, 59 l.y.

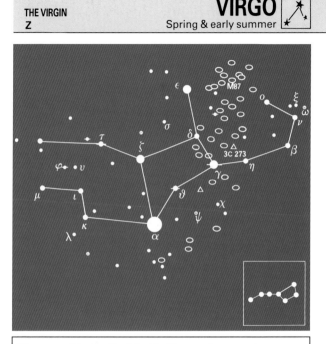

The curve of the handle of the Big Dipper points towards
Arcturus in Boötes, and if the curve is continued on it points
towards **Spica** in Virgo. **Porrima** is a famous double, two yellow-
white stars which can be distinguished in small telescopes. **Theta**
(θ) is a double of two blue-white stars of magnitudes 4.4 and 8.6;
they are 140 light years away.

The **Virgo cluster** of galaxies lies about 65 million light years
away. The brightest are visible as hazy patches in 150 mm
telescopes. **M 87** is a huge elliptical galaxy with more than 1000
globular clusters surrounding it. It is a radio source and is thought
to have a giant black hole at the center.

One of the brightest and best known quasars, **3C 273**, is in
Virgo. It looks like a 13th magnitude blue star and is estimated to
be about 3000 million light years away.

α (Spica) blue-white eclipsing binary, mag. 1, 260 l.y.: β yellow,
mag. 3.6, 33 l.y.: γ (Porrima), yellow-white double, mag. 2.8,
36 l.y.: δ red giant, mag. 3.4, 180 l.y.: ϵ yellow giant, mag. 2.8,
100 l.y.: ζ white, mag. 3.4, 1100 l.y.

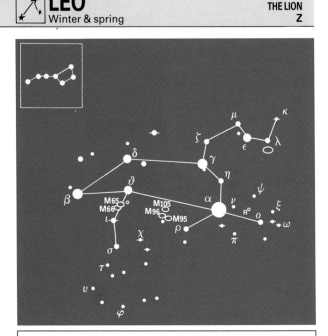

The stars of the pan of the Big Dipper converge on Leo. The constellation represents a lion crouching, with the sickle of stars on the right as its head.

Good double stars in Leo include **Gamma** (γ), a pair of golden yellow giants, visible in small telescopes and **Iota** (ι), a more difficult double to separate, needing a 150 mm telescope. **Regulus** has a wide companion visible in binoculars. **R Leo** is a Mira-type red giant variable which fluctuates from mag. 5.4 to 10.5 every 313 days; it is 3000 light years away.

The edge of the Virgo cluster of galaxies lies in Leo. In one small cluster, known as the Leo cluster, **M 65** and **M 66**, **M 95**, **M 96** and **M 105** are amongst the brightest, with magnitudes between 9 and 10.

α (Regulus) blue-white, mag. 1.4, 85 l.y.: β (Denebola) white, mag. 2.1, 42 l.y.: γ (Algieba) yellow giant double, mag. 2, 100 l.y.: δ (Zosma) blue-white, mag. 2.6, 52 l.y.: ϵ yellow giant, mag. 3, 310 l.y.: ζ white, mag. 3.4, 120 l.y.: ι yellow-white close double, mag. 4, 78 l.y.

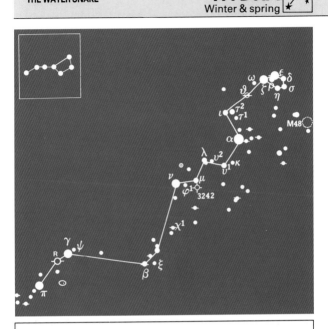

The largest constellation in the sky but faint and not easy to find, apart from the head and **Alphard**, the heart of the snake. It extends from the head, which lies just below the midpoint of a line drawn between Procyon in Canis Minor and Regulus in Leo, well into the southern hemisphere, to end near Centaurus. The head is formed of a lozenge of six stars, **Zeta** (ζ), **Epsilon** (ϵ), **Rho** (ρ), **Delta** (δ), **Sigma** (σ) and **Eta** (η).

M 48 is a rich open star cluster just visible to the naked eye on a dark night but not always easy to find. It can be seen more clearly with binoculars. It has about 80 stars and lies 3000 light years away.

NGC 3242 is a planetary nebula, sometimes said to resemble Jupiter. In binoculars it looks like a pale blue disk, revealing its ring form in a large telescope.

α (Alphard) orange giant, mag. 2, 130 l.y.: ν orange, mag. 3.1, 130 l.y.: ϵ double yellow and blue, mag. 3.4, 110 l.y.: ζ orange giant, mag. 3.1, 125 l.y.

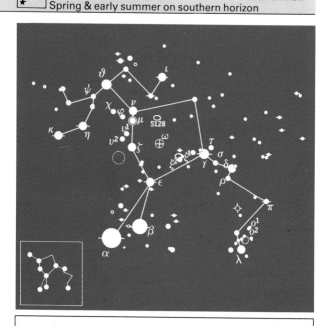

Only the upper parts of the constellation are visible from the northern hemisphere. **Alpha Centauri** (α), the closest star to our Sun, consists of two yellow stars which orbit each other every 80 years. **Proxima Centauri**, an 11th magnitude red dwarf smaller than Jupiter, orbits the other two.

Within the central figure of Centaurus, an irregular rectangle of five stars, is **Omega Centauri** (ω). This globular cluster is one of the brightest in the sky. Individual stars can be seen with binoculars. **NGC 5128** is a peculiar giant elliptical galaxy which appears in larger telescopes to have a band of dust around it. It has been identified as the radio source, **Centaurus A**, and it also emits X-rays. It probably has a massive black hole at the center.

α (Rigil Kentaurus) yellow double, mag. 0.27, 4.3 l.y.: β blue giant, mag. 0.6, 460 l.y.: γ blue-white double, mag. 2.2, 110 l.y.: θ orange, mag. 2.1, 46 l.y.: δ blue-white, mag. 2.6, 330 l.y.: ϵ blue-white, mag. 2.3, 490 l.y.: ζ blue-white, mag. 2.6, 360 l.y.: ν blue-white, mag. 3.4, 490 l.y.

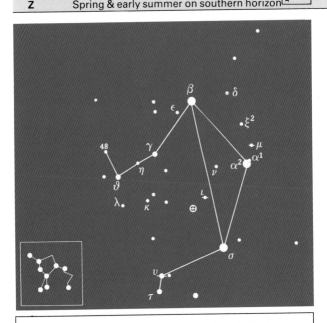

A line pointing towards the horizon, drawn through the right hand stars of Ophiuchus, points towards the faint zodiacal constellation of Libra. It lies between Antares in Scorpio and Spica in Virgo.

Libra was once part of the neighboring constellation of Scorpius; **Alpha** (α) and **Beta** (β) were the claws. Beta is unusual in that it is greenish in color. **Iota** (ι) is a multiple star with a blue-white primary of magnitude 4.5 and two faint 10th magnitude companions. They are only divisible in telescopes of 75 mm or more.

48 Libra is a blue giant star which rotates abnormally rapidly. In consequence it throws off a ring of gas, like Pleione in the Pleiades and Gamma (γ) Cassiopeiae. Such stars are called shell stars.

α blue-white with white companion, mag. 2.6, 72 l.y.: β greenish, mag. 2.6, 120 l.y.: σ red giant, mag. 3.3, 165 l.y.

The head of the Scorpion is visible low on the southeastern horizon in early summer in the higher northern latitudes but its sting is only visible from lower latitudes (south of 30°).

Antares is the brightest star in this part of the sky. It is a huge star, 300 times the diameter of the Sun. **Nu** (ν) is a quadruple star, with two double stars, a rare combination like the famous Double Double in Lyra. Telescopes of 100 mm or more are needed to split them completely. **Xi** (ξ) looks like another quadruple, but is actually a multiple star, with one member of the pairs itself a double, so that five stars are involved.

Many star fields and clusters, like clusters **M 6** and **M 7**, lie in the tail of Scorpius since it crosses the Milky Way. **M 4** is a large globular cluster visible in binoculars.

α (Antares) variable red supergiant, mag. 1, 330 l.y.: β blue-white double, mag. 2.7, 540 l.y.: σ blue-white giant, mag. 2.9, 590 l.y.: δ blue-white, mag. 2.3, 550 l.y.: ϵ orange giant, mag. 2.3, 70 l.y.: θ yellow-white supergiant, mag. 1.9, 910 l.y.: λ blue-white, mag. 1.6, 270 l.y.

The line of three stars in Aquila points towards Sagittarius which lies low on the southern horizon in early and mid summer in the northern hemisphere. Looking towards Sagittarius is also to look towards the center of the Milky Way, so the constellation is rich in star fields, nebulae and clusters.

Amongst the nebulae, famous examples include **M 8**, the **Lagoon Nebula**, to the naked eye an irregular hazy glow about the size of the full Moon. The eastern half contains the star cluster, **NGC 6530** which includes several T Tauri stars. The **Trifid Nebula**, **M 20**, is a cloud of glowing gas divided into three by dark dust lanes. It contains a central triple star.

M 22 is a globular cluster, the third brightest in the sky and easy to see in binoculars. It is approximately 10,000 light years away. **M 23**, an open cluster about 4500 light years away, is more diffuse.

ϵ blue-white, mag. 1.9, 85 l.y.: γ yellow giant, mag. 3, 120 l.y.: δ orange giant, mag. 2.7, 82 l.y.: σ blue-white, mag. 2, 210 l.y.: λ orange giant, mag. 2.8, 98 l.y.

A line drawn from Vega in Lyra through Altair in Aquila points southwards towards the horizon, and also points towards Capricornus. The constellation depicts a goat with the tail of a fish.

Alpha (α), also called Algedi, is a multiple star consisting of two unrelated stars. **Alpha One** is a yellow supergiant 120 light years away and **Alpha Two** a yellow giant 1600 light years away; the former shines with magnitude 3.6 and the latter with magnitude 4.2. Alpha One appears to have a wide 9th magnitude companion but the companion is actually unrelated. Alpha Two is a true double with an 11th magnitude companion which is itself double.

M 30 is a globular cluster with a dense center, visible in small telescopes.

β golden yellow, mag. 3.1, 250 l.y.: δ white, mag. 2.9, 49 l.y.: γ white, mag. 3.7, 100 l.y.

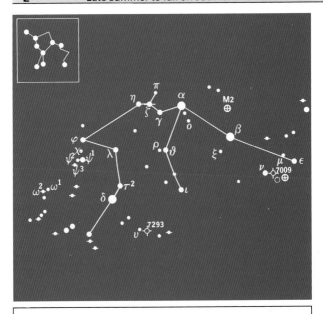

Aquarius represents a man pouring water from a jar. The most distinctive configuration in the constellation is the Y of four stars formed by **Eta** (η), **Zeta** (ζ), **Pi** (π) and **Gamma** (γ), which represents the water jar. The line of stars representing the wings of Cygnus point towards this Y-shape, as does the western of the two fishes in Pisces.

The **Saturn Nebula** (**NGC 7009**) is a planetary nebula that appears as a blue-green disk in small telescopes. At higher magnifications it resembles the planet Saturn. **NGC 7293**, the **Helix Nebula** is the largest in the sky but is not easy to see in the northern hemisphere. It appears as a misty circular patch in small telescopes, low in the southern sky in fall.

Several globular clusters are present in Aquarius, including **M 2**, one of the finest, visible in binoculars or small telescopes. It lies 50,000 light years away.

α yellow supergiant, mag. 3, 950 l.y.: β yellow supergiant, mag. 2.9, 980 l.y.: δ white giant, mag. 3.3, 98 l.y.: γ white, mag. 3.8, 91 l.y.: ζ white binary, mag. 3.6, 76 l.y.

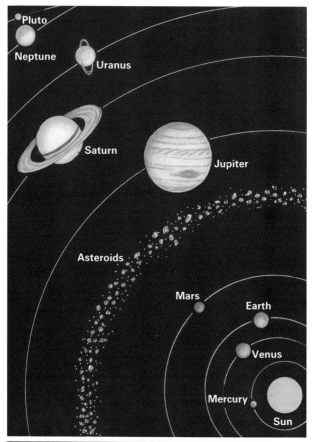

The Solar System lies in a spiral arm of our galaxy, the Milky Way, revolving around the galactic center about once every 225 million years. It consists of the Sun with nine planets in orbit around it, together with the moons orbiting the planets, asteroids, comets, meteoroids and dust. The planets are (in sequence from the center): Mercury, Venus, Earth, Mars, Jupiter, Saturn, Uranus, Neptune and Pluto.

The planets are not all similar in size or composition. The four inner planets, Mercury, Venus, Earth and Mars, are small, solid and rocky. Then come four giant gas planets, Jupiter, Saturn, Uranus and Neptune, which are formed mostly of hydrogen and helium. The outermost planet, Pluto is small and appears to be made of ice.

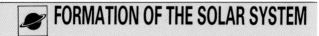

It is thought that the Solar System formed from a rotating cloud of gas, the Solar Nebula. As this cloud rotated it gradually increased its speed, and rotational and gravitational forces caused it to assume the form of a disk. In the center of this disk the gases condensed to form a protosun, until the matter was so dense that the temperature rose high enough to initiate thermonuclear reactions and the Sun then assumed its familiar form.

In the outer rings of the disk the planets were formed. It is not clear how this process occurred, but apparently nuclei developed which then grew into planets. Only a fraction of the material which had formed the original disk was gathered into the planets. The rest was dispersed into space.

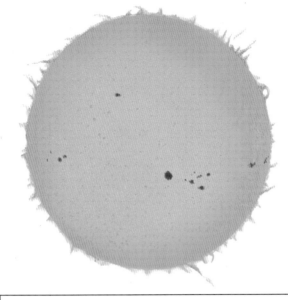

The Sun is a yellow star, with a diameter of 864,400 miles. It consists of a central core, surrounded by a radiative zone and a convective zone with an outer photosphere and a gaseous chromosphere. In the core, the temperature reaches 27 million °F and nuclear reactions occur, during which hydrogen is converted to helium and energy is released.

The core is surrounded by the other, much cooler layers in which nuclear reactions do not occur. In the innermost of these layers heat from the core is transported by radiation. The energy completes its journey upwards by huge convection cells into the top layer, the photosphere, a shining shell of gas which forms the surface of the Sun. It has a temperature of about 10,800 °F. From Earth the photosphere has a granular appearance created by the tops of the convection cells.

Outside the photosphere is the gaseous chromosphere; this layer contains jets of hot gases rising from the photosphere. The tops of the convection cells in the photosphere can be seen in the chromosphere as a network of circles. The chromosphere merges with the corona.

⭐ VIEWING THE SUN

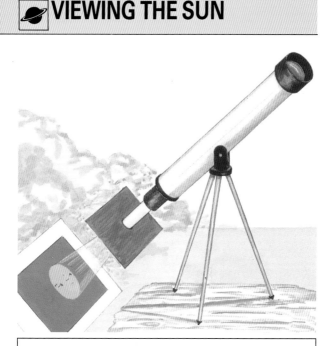

It is very dangerous to look at the Sun directly and looking at it through binoculars or a telescope can cause blindness. Even using a dark filter or a piece of negative film is not safe. The only safe way to view the Sun is to project its image through a telescope onto a piece of card. Another piece of card with a hole in it, around the eyepiece of the telescope will shade the card and make the image clearer.

The image will show that the Sun is darker at the edges than at the center, evidence of its gaseous nature, and that it has a granular appearance. The granules are each about 500 miles across and represent the tops of the huge convection cells that bring hot gases from deep inside the Sun into the photosphere.

The Sun is not uniform in its appearance. Active regions are localized magnetic fields which can develop quite quickly, building up in about 10 days. They appear as bright patches and are associated with dark sunspots, filaments and flares.

SUNSPOTS 🪐

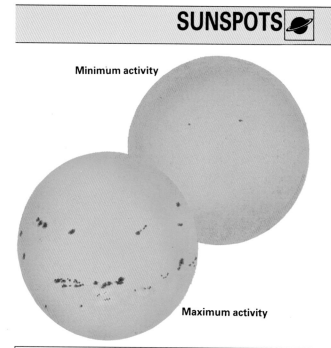

Minimum activity

Maximum activity

Sunspots are dark spots which appear in active regions, most often in pairs or groups. They are centers of intense magnetic activity. Of a pair of spots, one will be "north," the other "south" and there is a magnetic field between them like that around a magnet. They appear dark because they have a lower temperature than the photosphere. The center of a sunspot has a temperature of about 9000 °F, the lighter edge 10,000 °F.

Sunspots appear to move across the surface of the Sun but in reality they remain in the same position while the Sun rotates. They are thought to be caused by the "winding up" of the Sun's magnetic field by its uneven rotation. The number of sunspots varies in a cycle with the activity of the Sun, each peak of activity recurring about once every 11 years. The next such peak is due in about 1990. Sunspots first appear in latitudes 30–40° north and south and gradually move towards the equator, declining in activity as they go, until they decay. Remains of the old sunspot cycle may still be apparent at the equator while members of the new cycle are appearing at higher latitudes.

PROMINENCES

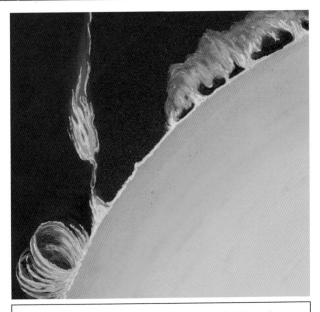

Prominences are large clouds of material extending above the chromosphere into the corona. They can be seen at the edge of the Sun during eclipses or, with special equipment, as dark filaments on the Sun's surface. They are the same color as the chromosphere and are associated with active regions.

There are two kinds of prominences. Quiescent prominences last for several months and may resemble hedgerows or arches. They form along the line separating the magnetic fields of two sunspots and may be 125,000 miles long and 25,000 miles high.

Active prominences form and change very rapidly, many lasting less than an hour. They may take the form of arches or loops, often rising very rapidly from the Sun's surface. They are often associated with flare activity.

In the active eruptive prominences material is thrown outwards from the chromosphere into the corona but in the longer lived loops and arches the material is condensing from the corona and flowing downwards into the chromosphere.

Flares occur in active regions, usually in areas where there are multiple sunspots. They are sudden violent releases of energy which last from a few minutes to a few hours, typically lasting about 20 minutes. Flares vary with the solar cycle, as do prominences and sunspots. Far more flares are produced at the peak of solar activity than in a quiescent phase. The radiated energy in a flare covers the whole range of the spectrum from gamma rays and hard X-rays to radio waves.

Electrons and photons are ejected from the Sun during flares; they move out into the corona and on outwards into space. They have an important effect on the Earth, producing spectacular polar lights and causing noise storms that interfere with radio reception.

Flares are rarely seen in white light. They need to be observed through a filter that allows light in the red part of the spectrum emitted by hydrogen gas to pass through it.

The corona is the Sun's outer atmosphere. It can be seen clearly during a total eclipse but is not normally visible from Earth. It consists of ionized gases (plasma) with a temperature varying from 1.8 to 9 million °F. However its density is very low so that it contains little real "heat." The high temperature of the corona has been a puzzle for many years since it cannot gain heat from the photosphere, which only has a temperature of 10,800 °F. It is thought that its energy comes from the magnetic fields in the active regions of the Sun, which release energy into the solar atmosphere.

The corona varies with the solar cycle. During quiescent periods the corona can be seen to have streamers directed away from the Sun in a pattern like that shown by a magnet. During peak activity the corona is brighter and has many coronal holes, with loops and arches above prominences and flares. Coronal holes are dark patches in the corona with a lower temperature. Out of these holes stream the solar wind, high speed streams of electrons and protons. The solar wind affects the magnetic fields of the planets, including that of Earth.

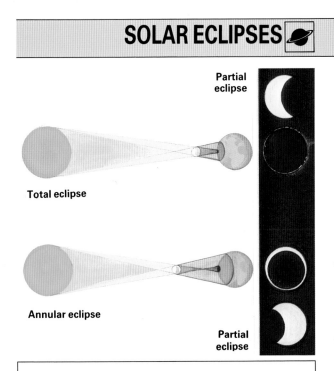

Partial
eclipse

Total eclipse

Annular eclipse

Partial
eclipse

A solar eclipse occurs when the Moon passes between the Earth
and the Sun and its shadow touches the Earth. A total eclipse
occurs within the area of the umbra, when the Moon totally covers
the Sun. This area passes as a track along the surface of the Earth,
a track which is not more than 169 miles wide. On either side of
this track the moon only partly covers the Sun and in this
penumbra region the eclipse is only partial.

During an eclipse the Moon's shadow gradually creeps across
the face of the Sun. At the last moment, before the Sun is covered,
a flash of light may appear, giving what is known as the "diamond
ring effect." This is the light of the Sun shining through a valley
on the edge of the Moon. When the Moon has covered the Sun the
chromosphere, corona and prominences become visible and may
be viewed safely.

In a total eclipse the Moon and Sun appear to be the same size
in the sky. However in an annular eclipse, the Moon is at its
furthest from Earth when it passes between Earth and Sun, and
the umbra of its shadow does not touch the Earth. The Sun
appears as a ring around the Moon during the eclipse.

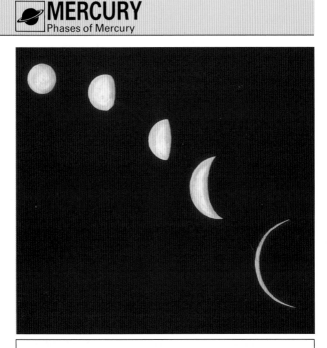

Mercury is the closest of the planets to the Sun. It has the most eccentric orbit of all the planets except Pluto. At perihelion it approaches to within 28,500,000 miles of the Sun while at aphelion it is 43,300,000 miles away from the Sun. It completes one orbit in 88 Earth days and rotates on its axis once every 58½ Earth days. This means that any point on the surface of Mercury is subjected to long periods of heat or cold. The temperature at midday may reach 650 °F while at night it drops to −270 °F.

Mercury is very difficult to see from Earth since it is so close to the Sun. It is best looked for low in the sky before dawn and after sunset but even then it only appears briefly. Mercury has phases like the Moon, is new when it is between Earth and the Sun and is full when behind the Sun. It is best seen when it is three quarters full.

Mercury is the smallest of the four inner planets with a diameter of 3030 miles at the equator, less than half the size of the Earth. It has no moons.

Mercury is a rocky planet, probably with a core of iron and an outer mantle of silicate rock like the Earth. It has virtually no atmosphere but does have a magnetic field and traps some helium from the solar wind. It is similar in appearance to the Moon, with a very heavily cratered surface. It is thought that the large craters are all about 4,000–4,500 million years old and were produced soon after the formation of the planets. The smaller craters were all formed later. Evidence for this theory lies in the fact that the small craters are always superimposed on the large ones.

The Caloris Basin is the largest single feature known on the surface of Mercury, at the present time. However there has only been one space probe, Mariner 10, which approached Mercury close enough to photograph it and it only viewed part of the surface. The Caloris Basin is a large basin, with a diameter of 800 miles, and has been compared to the Mare Imbrium on the Moon. Surrounding it is a rim of mountains and extending outwards from these is a radial network of ridges and valleys. The floor of the Basin is extensively fractured.

Venus is the second planet out from the Sun, the closest of the planets to Earth, and is the brightest object in the sky apart from the Sun and Moon. When viewed from Earth it appears as a bright star in the west after sunset (the Evening Star) or in the east before sunrise (the Morning Star). It has phases like the Moon, appearing new when between the Earth and Sun and full when on the far side of the Sun.

Venus has a nearly circular orbit, about 67,200,000 miles out from the Sun and it completes one revolution in about 225 Earth days. Venus rotates slowly, only once every 243 Earth days, so its day is longer than its year. It rotates on its axis from east to west, in the opposite direction to the Sun and to most of the planets. Venus has no moons.

It is about the same size as Earth with a diameter of 7,516 miles but has a very different climate. It has a surface temperature of about 870 °F, the result of its carbon dioxide atmosphere which has acted as a heat trap for solar radiation and its dense clouds. The atmospheric pressure at the surface is about 90 times as high as that on Earth.

Venus appears very bright from space, the result of sunlight reflected off the thick clouds. Venus has a very thick, dense atmosphere, with cloud tops about 60 miles above the surface. The atmosphere is composed mostly of carbon dioxide with small amounts of nitrogen, oxygen, sulfur dioxide and water vapor. The clouds are formed of liquid and solid sulfur particles and of droplets of sulfuric acid; this makes investigation of the Venusian atmosphere very difficult. Cloud cover extends down to about 25 miles of the surface, below this level the air is clear. The light is like that of a dull winter's day in northern latitudes on Earth. Only about 2% of the incident sunlight penetrates through the clouds.

Near the surface of Venus there is very little wind and the dense air moves sluggishly. However at the top of the atmosphere high winds, travelling at 150 miles per hour from east to west, sweep the clouds around the planet once every four Earth days. This high velocity cloud system is powered by solar radiation which cannot penetrate into the atmosphere, so that the Sun's energy is absorbed in the cloud tops.

VENUS

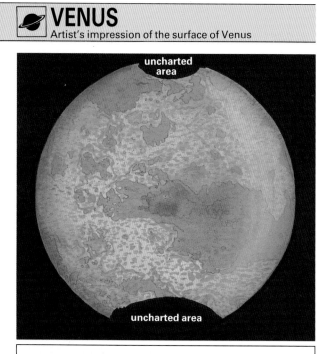

The surface of Venus is rocky and much of it is comparatively smooth, probably because in the intense heat the rocks are deformed and plasticized. It consists mostly of a rolling plain which covers about 70% of the surface.

There are also several highland areas, covering about 10% of the surface. In the northern hemisphere there is a high mountainous plateau called Ishtar Terra, about the size of Australia. Another highland plateau area, called Aphrodite Terra, is found on the equator; it is about the size of Africa. It has mountains in the east and west and a lower central region; in it there is also a huge chasm like the African rift valley, called the Diana chasm, which is 175 miles wide and 2½ miles deep. Another highland region, Beta Regio, contains two volcanoes which might still be active.

Depressions and basins cover the other 20% of Venus, the biggest of which is Atalanta Planitia. This is in the northern hemisphere and is about a mile deep.

The Earth is the third planet out from the Sun. It is really one of a pair of planets—a binary system—with the Moon. It orbits the Sun at a mean distance of 92,955,630 miles and takes 365.25 days to complete one orbit. Its rotation period (day) is 23 hr 56 min 4 secs. It is the largest of the four inner planets, with an equatorial diameter of 7,926 miles.

Viewed from space the Earth appears blue, brown and green, with a pattern of white clouds. At any one time about 50% of the Earth's surface is covered by clouds which are formed of water vapor. Its seasons depend on its axial inclination—its tilt. In summer in the northern hemisphere the north pole is tilted towards the Sun while at the same time the south pole is tilted away from the Sun and experiences winter.

The Earth has a strong magnetic field which interacts with the solar wind and traps charged particles from it, to form the Van Allen Belts. They form a potential hazard to spacecraft since they affect electronic equipment.

The Earth is the only planet known which supports life. This is due to the presence of an atmosphere of 76% nitrogen and 21% oxygen with carbon dioxide in small amounts, and a temperature range that allows water to exist as a liquid and as a gas. Giant cycles of activity occur in the atmosphere, circulating the water and carbon dioxide and creating the familiar weather patterns. The cycles depend not only on solar radiation but also on the oceans and the plant life.

The atmosphere is divided into several zones from the surface zone to the rarified exosphere, over 250 miles up. In the ionosphere, a zone in the upper atmosphere, most of the atoms and molecules are ionized. This layer reflects radio waves and allows radio communication around the planet. However solar flares disrupt the layer and make radio reception difficult.

In the ozone layer, between 10 and 30 miles up, oxygen exists as ozone, an effect produced by solar radiation which breaks oxygen down into its atoms. The ozone layer protects the Earth from harmful ultraviolet light which would cause cancer and mutations in life forms.

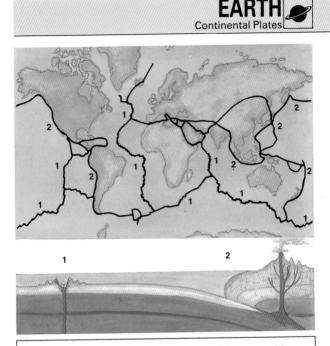

The Earth consists of a central liquefied nickel-iron core with a temperature of about 7200 °F, covered by a hot thick silicate mantle. This is covered by a thin rocky crust which is broken into about 15 plates. Some of these form oceanic plates beneath the oceans and others form continental plates. The Earth is covered by about 70% ocean.

There are mountain ridges in the middle of the oceans where the oceanic plates meet (1). Along these ridges magma from the mantle rises up and spreads laterally to produce sea floor spreading—the Atlantic may spread by as much as four inches per year. Along the ocean edges the oceanic plates meet the continental plates and slide beneath them (2); the enormous pressures produce mountain chains like the Rockies and Andes.

The interaction of the 15 plates has created the present configuration of the Earth's oceans and continents. But they were not always the same and the continents have moved extensively since the Earth was formed. Today, for example, the Red Sea is widening at the rate of half an inch per year as Africa is moving diagonally away from Arabia.

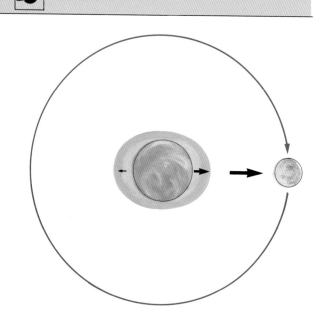

Ocean tides are caused by the pull of the Moon and the Sun but the Moon's influence is greater because it is closer. The Moon's pull produces a bulge in the ocean beneath it causing a high tide. At the same time a corresponding bulge and high tide occurs on the far side of the Earth since the Moon's influence is weakest at that point. The bulges move around the Earth as it rotates, producing two high tides and two low tides in just over a day.

When the Sun is in line with the Moon (at new and full moons) it reinforces the gravitational pull, producing spring tides. When the Moon and the Sun are at right angles, the gravitational pull of the Sun partially cancels out that of the Moon, producing neap tides.

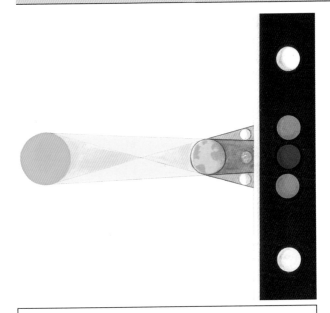

A lunar eclipse occurs when the Earth passes between the Sun and Moon. The eclipse is visible from one whole Earth hemisphere. The Moon first passes into the penumbra region of the Earth's shadow. At this time its light is dimmed but its face is not obscured.

Once the Moon begins to pass into the umbra, then the shadow of the Earth can be seen, at first as a thin line across one side of the Moon, then creeping slowly across the face of the Moon, until the whole is darkened if the eclipse is total. If the Sun, Earth and Moon do not line up exactly, the eclipse is only partial.

The Moon is a satellite of the Earth, revolving round it once every 27.3 days. Since it also turns on its axis once in the same time, it always keeps the same face turned towards the Earth. The orbit of the Moon is eccentric; at its closest approach it is 221,330 miles from the Earth, at its furthest it is 252,548 miles away.

The Moon does not shine with light of its own, but only with reflected sunlight. The Moon's phases, increasing from New Moon to Full and then decreasing back to Old Moon, change with its position in its orbit. When it is exactly between the Sun and the Earth it is unlit and cannot be seen from Earth—it is then said to be New. As it moves along its path, a thin crescent of light appears along one edge and gradually increases as the Moon waxes. At the first quarter, half the Moon can be seen from Earth and the Moon is a quarter of the way round its orbit. At Full Moon it is on the opposite side of the Earth from the Sun and from then on its sunlit face decreases or wanes until only the Old Crescent can be seen, on the opposite side of its face to the New Moon.

There are three quite distinct kinds of terrain on the Moon, which can all be seen from the Earth. There are the charcoal gray plains or *maria* which occupy about 15% of the surface, there are the mountainous highland areas which cover about 85% of the Moon and there are the walled craters.

The *maria* give the distinctive look to the face of the Moon. They were deep basins which were filled with lava during a period when the Moon was active volcanically. This lava has set into flat, relatively unmarked plains with a dark gray color, darker than the surrounding areas.

The mountainous highland areas occupy almost the entire far side of the Moon and they also surround the *maria* on the near side. These mountains are the oldest parts of the Moon and they have been bombarded with meteors and dust particles from space since they were formed. They are studded with craters, fragmented into rubble in many areas and split by faults. Some of the peaks are very high, as high as or higher than the Rockies, and since the Moon is so much smaller than Earth, these are very high mountains.

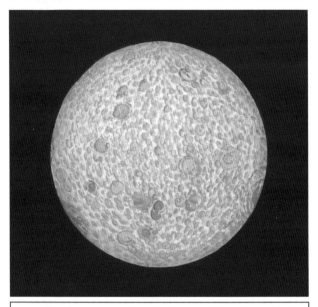

Craters are found all over the Moon, evidence of its lack of atmosphere and continuous bombardment from space. They are formed when a meteor crashes into the Moon. Most craters consist of a deep depression surrounded by a wall; they often have a central peak. Ray craters are visible from Earth; they have long rays or lines which extend outwards from their walls, sometimes for great distances on the Moon's surface. They are best seen when the Moon is fully illuminated. Tycho, low down in the southern hemisphere is one such ray crater. In the *maria* there are relatively few walled craters but many ghost craters which have been filled with lava.

The rocks of the Moon are dark gray in color, even though it appears silvery when viewed from Earth. The charcoal gray lava flows of the *maria* are darker still. The whole surface of the Moon is coated with a layer of rock fragments and smaller "soil" particles. The layer may be several feet deep in the highlands or as little as a few inches. It has formed as a result of the continual bombardment by missiles from space of the lunar surface.

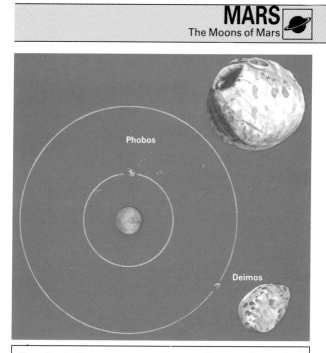

From Earth, Mars appears as a red-orange planet, outshone only by Venus and Jupiter; it is visible from Earth for several months each year. It is the furthest out of the four small inner planets, with an eccentric orbit; at perihelion it approaches to within 128,000,000 miles of the Sun, at aphelion it is 155,000,000 miles away. It takes 687 earth days to complete one orbit. It is a small planet, only 4200 miles in diameter at the equator and has a low density.

Mars has two small moons, Phobos and Deimos. Phobos, the inner moon is only 5830 miles from Mars, Deimos is 14,600 miles out. Both are probably ex-asteroids which have been captured by Mars, they are irregular in shape; Phobos is 17 miles across, Deimos 9 miles across.

Mars rotates once every 24 hr 37 min 22.6 sec and is inclined on its axis at an angle of about 24°; this tilt gives it seasons like that of Earth. Mars is a colder world than Earth, temperatures rarely climbing above freezing even in summer and dropping to a low point of −169 °F before dawn. At the poles temperatures stay below −189 °F throughout the year.

The atmosphere on Mars is thin, being equivalent to that on Earth at 185 miles up. It consists of 95% carbon dioxide with 5% nitrogen and argon. There are only traces of water vapor and oxygen. At perihelion, with the rise in temperature, dust storms often develop with the high winds which blow at that time. These may envelope the whole planet, obscuring its surface totally.

Mars has two white polar regions while the rest of the planet is dusky red in color. The northern ice cap in summer is formed mostly of water ice while the southern ice cap is dry ice (frozen carbon dioxide). In winter these frozen areas are enlarged by the addition of layers of dry ice when carbon dioxide freezes directly out of the cold air.

The northern and southern hemispheres are not the same; in the south the land is high and pock-marked with craters as well as criss-crossed by complex channels and gully systems. In the north the land is generally lower. To the south of the north pole are vast dunes, areas of wind-blown sand like the Sahara Desert.

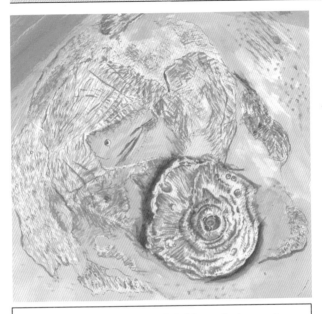

In contrast to the generally low relief of the north, there are two areas just north of the equator, Tharsis (which is about the size of Africa) and the smaller Elysium, in which the land rises so much these two areas appear as distinct bulges in the planet's spherical outline. In these regions there are several huge extinct volcanoes. Olympus mons, in Tharsis, is probably the biggest volcano in the Solar System; it towers over 15 miles above the surface of Mars and has a multiple caldera, 50 miles across. It is surrounded by hundreds of miles of lava flows. Surrounding Tharsis and Elysium are vast areas of radiating fractures, probably formed during the elevation of the regions.

To the east of Tharsis is a giant network of valleys and canyons which extends eastwards for 2500 miles, to end in chaotic terrain, a region of jumbled rocks and channels. Martian channels do not run in straight lines (in contrast to what was once thought) but form huge networks in several areas, suggesting that at one time there was extensive flooding. Today Mars is dry. There is no evidence of life on the planet.

THE ASTEROIDS

Jupiter

Mars

Asteroids

The asteroids are small rocky planetoids that mostly orbit between Mars and Jupiter. Over 2500 are known and thousands more too small to see are present in the Asteroid Belt. The largest known today is Ceres, with a diameter of about 620 miles. Asteroids probably formed at the same time as the rest of the Solar System. They vary from carbonaceous types which mostly orbit close to Jupiter, to siliceous types which mostly orbit closer to Mars.

Asteroids are not distributed evenly but in clusters (or families) and there are several gaps, the Kirkwood Gaps, within the Asteroid Belt. As well as those of the main belt, other groups of asteroids are found on other orbits in the Solar System. The Trojans are two clusters with the same orbit as Jupiter but one cluster remains 60° behind the giant planet while the other cluster orbits 60° ahead. Other asteroids have more eccentric orbits, one group crossing the path of Mars and approaching the Earth, and another group, known as Apollos, crossing the Earth's orbit. Chiron is a strange asteroid that orbits the Sun between Saturn and Uranus.

Jupiter is the fifth planet out from the Sun, a gas giant and the largest planet in the Solar System. It is enormous, with a volume more than a thousand times greater than Earth. Jupiter is not spherical, being flattened at the poles; its diameter at the equator is 88,680 miles but its polar diameter is only 83,340 miles. It rotates differentially, its equatorial regions rotating once in just under 10 hours while higher latitudes take about 5 minutes longer to complete one rotation.

At the cloud tops Jupiter is very cold, about −240 °F but pressure and temperature increase rapidly inside, reaching about 54,000 °F and 100 million atmospheres at the center. It is thought that Jupiter has a small core of silicates and iron, surrounded by a layer in which hydrogen is compressed into a metallic form by the high pressures. Outside this layer hydrogen exists as a liquid and the outer layers (beginning about 600 miles deep) consist of gaseous hydrogen and helium.

Jupiter's orbit is eccentric; at perihelion it approaches to within 460,000,000 miles of the Sun while at aphelion it is 506,500,000 miles away. One orbit takes 11.86 Earth years.

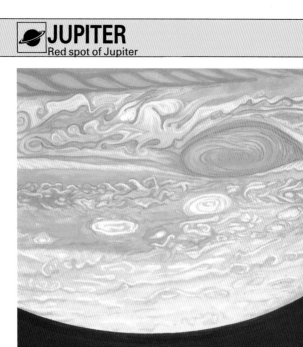

Viewed from Earth, Jupiter is outshone only by Venus. It appears as a bright planet in the sky for several months each year. With the aid of a small telescope it can be seen to be banded horizontally in light and dark zones of white, yellow and brown which are constantly changing. These are clouds moving rapidly across the planet with its rapid rotation; the banded effect is created by alternating flows of west and east currents. Rising clouds of ammonia crystals floating in hydrogen form the white bands. The darker bands of orange and brown are zones where the gases are descending back down into the atmosphere again.

Turbulence and high winds disturb the clouds and make constantly changing patterns of swirls, chevrons, plumes and spots. The Great Red Spot in the southern hemisphere is a gigantic whirling storm, its red color caused probably by phosphine. It is 16,270 miles long and 8,570 miles wide at present, but varies and seems to have got smaller since it was first discovered in the 17th century. Several oval white spots are also present in the southern hemisphere.

THE MOONS OF JUPITER

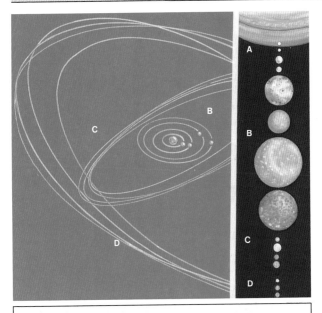

Jupiter has 16 known moons or satellites, four large inner moons and two groups of small outer moons; there are also several small inner moons (**A**) orbiting inside the large ones. The four large inner moons are named Galileans (**B**), after Galileo who detected them in 1610. They are like small planets in size.

The eight outer satellites are much smaller and may be captured asteroids. One group of four, Leda, Himalia, Lysithea and Elara (**C**), circle the planet about 7 million miles out. The other group, Ananke, Carme, Pasiphae and Sinope (**D**) have eccentric orbits, influenced by the Sun and with a mean distance of 13 million miles from Jupiter. Their motion is retrograde.

The small innermost satellites, Amalthea, Metis, Adrastea and Thebe (1) orbit closer to Jupiter than Io. These small moons are close to the Roche limit—the distance they can approach Jupiter without being pulled apart by its gravity.

Jupiter was discovered to have rings on the Voyager mission. However they are formed of dust and rock particles, unlike Saturn's ice rings and are not visible from Earth.

THE GALILEANS
Jupiter not drawn to scale

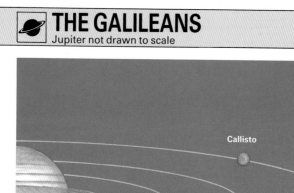

The Galileans are the four large inner moons of Jupiter. They are called Io, Europa, Ganymede and Callisto. They all have synchronous orbits, like our own Moon they rotate in the same time that they take to complete one orbit and so always have the same face turned towards Jupiter. All are visible with a telescope from the Earth and can be seen to transit across the face of Jupiter. However, little was known of them until the Voyager missions. These Voyager space probes, which investigated the moons, were designed to cope with high levels of radiation since the inner three moons fall within the magnetic field of Jupiter and are constantly bombarded with radiation, high energy protons and electrons. A flux tube of electrons and ions connects Jupiter and Io.

Io is the innermost of the four, orbiting once every 42½ hours at a mean distance of 261,800 miles from Jupiter. Europa orbits about once every 3½ Earth days, at a mean distance of 416,600 miles. Ganymede orbits once every 7 Earth days, 4 hours at a mean distance of 664,500 miles. Callisto orbits in 16¾ Earth days at a mean distance of 1,169,000 miles from Jupiter.

Io

Diameter: 2260 miles. Close to Jupiter & affected by Europa, Io is subjected to severe gravitational & tidal stresses & has active volcanoes as a result. Appears to have a red sulfur & sulfur dioxide crust over a molten silicate interior.

Europa

Diameter: 1941 miles. White & thought to be covered in water ice. No craters but surface covered by system of cracks & markings. May be partly melted ice or liquid water beneath surface, which wells through the cracks & freezes.

Ganymede

Diameter: 3276 miles, largest Solar System moon. A surface of ice & rock, 60 miles thick, covers a mantle of slushy ice. Surface varies from dark, heavily cratered areas to lighter areas which exhibit "bundles" of parallel grooves.

Callisto

Diameter: 2993 miles. Only Galilean moon outside Jupiter's radiation belt. Darkest of four & most difficult to see from Earth. Similar to Ganymede with an ice & rock surface 100–200 miles thick, over mantle of slushy ice. Heavily cratered but without parallel grooves.

Saturn is the sixth planet out from the Sun, the second largest in the Solar System with an equatorial diameter of 74,500 miles. It is also the lightest and least dense, with a density less than water—it would float! Saturn has an eccentric orbit, reaching 936 million miles away from the Sun at aphelion and approaching to within 853 million miles at perihelion. It completes one orbit in about 29½ Earth years.

Like Jupiter, Saturn is a gas giant and is flattened at the poles. It rotates rapidly, once every 10 hrs 39 mins, moving faster at the equator than at the poles. However, unlike Jupiter, Saturn is inclined at an angle and therefore exhibits seasons. Its temperature at its cloud tops is approximately −290 °F but at any one time one pole is turned towards the Sun and is warmer than the other by a few degrees. Saturn has a similar internal structure to Jupiter, with a small core, surrounded by metallic hydrogen, liquid hydrogen and a deep turbulent atmosphere of hydrogen and helium. Its core temperature and pressure are lower, however, 21,600 °F and 8 million atmospheres.

Saturn not to scale

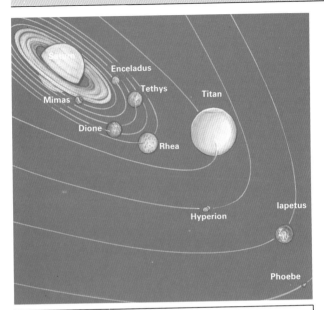

Viewed from Earth Saturn appears like a bright star, slow-moving and less brilliant than the other closer planets. It is circled around the equator by a series of bright rings, which make it quite unmistakeable when Saturn is viewed through a telescope. Since the planet and rings are inclined at 27° to its orbit, the angle at which we see them from Earth varies as Saturn orbits the Sun. Saturn appears to vary in brightness, being brightest when the rings are tilted towards the Earth, dimmest when the rings are edge on to the Earth. The rings are tilted towards the Earth at intervals of 13.75 and 15.75 years, the difference being due to Saturn's eccentric orbit, and will next present in this position in 1989.

Saturn is yellowish in color and, although banded, the bands are obscured by haze. They are less obvious and much more uniform than the bands of Jupiter, even though they are caused by similar conditions. There are no major semi-permanent features like spots or plumes on Saturn's surface although small features may appear for a few days at a time.

Cassini Division

Saturn is encircled by a series of rings. They gird the equator of the planet which is tilted at an angle of 27°; the rings are similarly tilted. They measure 170,800 miles across and consist of three separate bands. The two outer rings are bright and are separated by a dark division (the Cassini division) which contains few particles. The innermost or dusky ring is semi-transparent; hence it is called the crepe ring.

The rings are formed of ice particles arranged in thousands of individual ringlets. The size of the particles ranges from dust fragments to chunks like large rocks. Various theories have been put forward to account for the rings but it is probable that they were formed with Saturn itself.

THE MOONS OF SATURN

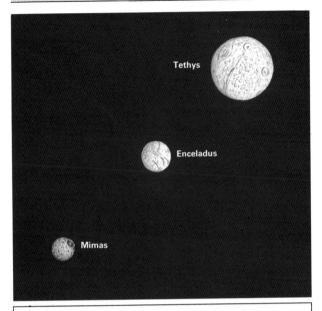

Saturn has 21 moons, one large one the size of a small planet (Titan) and the others very much smaller. All but one circle the planet more or less in the equatorial plane. Little was known of the moons until the Voyager fly-bys. Of the small satellites, Rhea and Iapetus are the largest, with diameters of 950 miles and 890 miles respectively. The smallest is Phoebe with a diameter of 100 miles. All are formed largely of ice but they vary greatly in density and in appearance.

Mimas, the innermost moon, circles Saturn at a mean distance of 115,250 miles and completes one orbit in about 22½ hours. It is notable for the one enormous crater on its northern hemisphere, which is 80 miles in diameter, a third of the diameter of Mimas itself. Enceladus, the second satellite, has few small craters and may be covered with soft slushy ice which covers any craters as they are formed. Tethys, third moon out, seems to be almost pure ice; it has a unique feature, a huge trench running from north pole to south pole; it also has several huge craters.

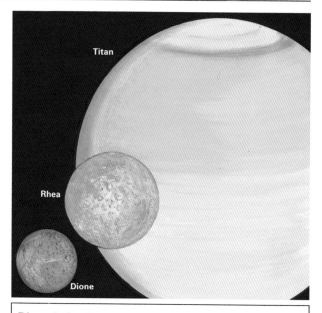

Dione, the fourth moon, is the densest of the small moons and has a system of bright, wispy frost-like features, which are probably faults, on the otherwise dark trailing hemisphere. In the center of this feature is the crater Amata, and other craters are also present. Rhea, the fifth moon, is similar to Dione with less prominent bright wispy features and many craters.

Titan is the second largest moon in the Solar System, second only to Ganymede and larger than the planet Mercury. It can be seen from Earth through a telescope when it resembles a small star. Very little is known about it for its surface is completely obscured by orange-red clouds. It has a thick atmosphere of nitrogen with methane. Titan is the sixth moon out from Saturn, circling it at a distance of 758,600 miles. It is 3,200 miles in diameter and has a surface temperature of $-270\,°F$. At this temperature methane exists as a liquid, it freezes at $-295\,°F$ and boils at $-247\,°F$. It is thought that rivers and oceans of methane may exist on Titan, with methane rain falling from the clouds.

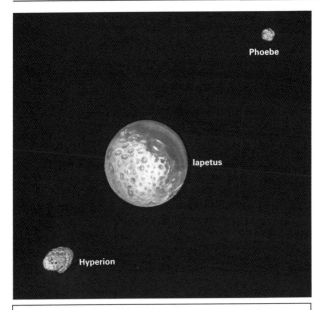

Hyperion, the seventh moon, differs from all other Saturn moons for it is irregular in shape and dark in color, with several craters. Iapetus, the eighth moon, has an unusual appearance, light and icy on the trailing hemisphere, covered with some kind of dark material on its leading hemisphere; this seems to have been extruded on to the moon's surface from inside. Iapetus' orbit is inclined to the ring-plane, unlike those of the other satellites orbiting Saturn in the equatorial plane.

Phoebe, the outermost of the moons, has a retrograde orbit, inclined at 150° to the ring plane. It is thought to be a captured asteroid, is dark in color and does not have synchronous rotation, in contrast to the other moons.

Uranus is the seventh planet out from the Sun, ranging in distance from 1,698 million miles out at perihelion to 1,865 million miles out at aphelion. It takes just over 84 Earth years to complete one orbit. It is a gas giant with a diameter of 32,200 miles and rotates once on its axis in 17.24 hours.

Uranus has an inclination unlike that of any other planet in the Solar System. It lies on its side with its south pole facing the Sun. It is thought that this orientation may be the result of a collision with a planet-sized body early in its history. Uranus has nine narrow, elliptical rings around its equator. The rings are dark, probably because the particles are formed of or coated with a material rich in carbon.

Uranus has a rocky core surrounded by a deep, dense hydrogen atmosphere in which clouds of frozen water, methane and ammonia are suspended. Towards the top of the atmosphere methane clouds predominate, giving Uranus its blue-green color when it is viewed from Earth or from space. From Earth Uranus is best seen with a telescope, appearing as a blue-green disk moving slowly across the sky.

Since Voyager passed Uranus in 1986, the planet is known to have 15 moons, ten small inner ones which mostly orbit just outside the rings and five large outer moons. The inner moons lie inside Uranus' magnetic field and are dark in color.

The five outer moons are Miranda, Ariel, Umbriel, Titania and Oberon. They are dark gray in color, formed of rock and ice, heavily cratered and two of them, Ariel and Titania show signs of volcanic activity. Both these moons have complex patterns of rift valleys on their surfaces.

The innermost moon, Miranda, is the smallest and the strangest. It is 300 miles in diameter and its surface is a dark rolling cratered plain, embedded in which are huge ovoid areas, 100–200 miles across, consisting of bright parallel ridges and scarps, often set at strange angles to each other. It is thought that the plains are rock and the ovoids ice.

Miranda orbits at 81,000 miles: Ariel (diam. 720 miles) orbits at 119,100 miles; Umbriel (diam. 740 miles) orbits at 165,900 miles; Titania (diam. 990 miles) orbits at 272,000 miles; Oberon (diam. 990 miles) orbits at 364,100 miles out.

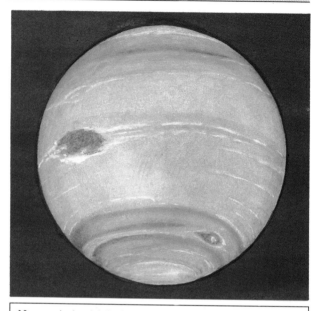

Neptune is the eighth planet out from the Sun, orbiting the Sun once every 164.8 Earth years. It has an almost circular orbit, with a mean distance from the Sun of 2,792 million miles. It is a gas giant with an equatorial diameter of 30,700 miles and a rotation period of 16 hrs 03 mins.

Till 1989, Neptune was known only as a blue-green disk in a telescope, but since Voyager II passed the planet in that year much more is known. Like the other gas giants, Neptune possesses a rocky core surrounded by a dense atmosphere of hydrogen, helium and methane. Its atmosphere is now known to be turbulent, with light and dark striations indicating rapid movement, and a massive storm (like Jupiter's Great Red Spot), known as the Great Dark Spot. Parallel banks of silvery cirrus clouds were also seen 30 miles above the outer layer.

Neptune has four narrow rings around its equator. Using a powerful telescope they were detected as broken arcs (incomplete rings would have been unique), but are now known to be complete rings formed of dust and debris with some areas more dense and reflective than others.

THE MOONS OF NEPTUNE

Triton

Nereid

Before Voyager II passed by, only two moons had been detected circling Neptune. It is now known to have eight, Triton and Nereid, the original two, and six new ones. The new moons are little more than large lumps of rock circling the planet near the equatorial plane; the largest is only 125 miles across.

Triton is large, with a diameter of about 2200 miles and it circles close to Neptune, about 220,000 miles out, completing one orbit about once every six days. Its orbit is retrograde (in the opposite direction to other moons in the Solar System) and tilted at about 20 degrees to the equatorial plane. Because of this, it is thought that Triton may not always have been a moon but perhaps once was a separate planet like Pluto. Triton is pinkish, with poles covered by frozen methane and nitrogen, and a surface deformed by ancient volcanic activity.

Nereid is very different, with a highly eccentric orbit, more like that of a comet than of a moon. It approaches to within 87,000 miles of Neptune at its closest, and reaches 5,900,000 miles out at its furthest point. It is small, about 300 miles across and resembles an asteroid.

For much of its orbiting cycle of 248 years, Pluto is the farthest planet from the Sun. However, its orbit is highly eccentric, reaching 4,580 million miles out at aphelion and approaching to within 2,748 million miles of the Sun at perihelion. It reaches this point in 1989. For the ten years either side of perihelion it is closer to the Sun than Neptune. However there is no danger of a collision since Pluto's orbit is inclined at an angle of 17°.

Pluto cannot be seen from Earth with the naked eye or even with a small telescope. It can be seen as a point of light with an 8-inch telescope. It is a very small planet, only 1500 miles in diameter, with a very low density. This low density suggests that it is probably formed of water ice.

Pluto has a moon, Charon, which has an equatorial diameter of about 600 miles. Charon completes one orbit around Pluto in 6.3 days, the same time it takes the planet to rotate once. To an observer on Pluto, therefore, Charon would appear to be stationary in the sky. The two bodies are only 10,500 miles apart.

Comets orbit the Sun, but unlike the planets they have highly elliptical orbits. Many have orbital periods so long and journey so far outside the Solar System that their return cannot be predicted. Others have elliptical orbits within the Solar System and return to perihelion every few years. These are known as Short Period Comets.

Comets have a nucleus consisting of frozen water, methane, carbon dioxide and rock particles, surrounded by dust and gas. When the comet approaches the Sun, dust and gas molecules are blown backwards along the comet's path forming a tail. This gives the comet its typical appearance as seen from Earth, with a bright head and a long drawn out tail which may stretch for millions of miles. Short Period Comets generally do not have tails—they have lost their gas and dust particles in their frequent passages round the Sun. Sometimes more than one tail is formed, one of gas and the other of dust.

Comets are named for their discoverers. The most famous is Halley's Comet which returns to the inner Solar System every 74–78 years, the last return being in 1986.

METEORS

Meteor showers are seen regularly on Earth, the most well-known being the Perseid shower that illuminates the night sky between July 27 and August 17 each year. They are produced by meteoroids, fragments of rock and dust found in the Solar System. When they enter the Earth's atmosphere they burn up with the friction and glow as meteors for a second or less.

Meteors may be single and unpredictable or they may occur in showers, appearing every year or once every few years. These meteor showers are remnants of comet tails. As the Earth passes through the orbit of a comet long gone, fragments of dust remaining from its tail burn up as meteors. Since they are moving in a definite path, a meteor shower will always appear to come from the same point in the sky. Thus the Perseids come from Perseus, the Lyrids (which appear in April) come from Lyra, the Taurids (which appear in late October and November) come from Taurus. Often the original comet is known; the Perseids come from Comet P/Swift-Tuttle which returns to the inner Solar System once every 33 years.

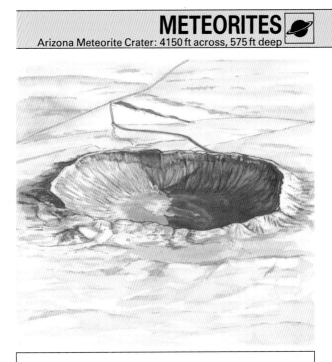

At irregular intervals (several have been recorded this century) larger chunks of material approach or crash into the Earth. These are meteorites and they are too large to burn up in their transit through the atmosphere. They reach the surface, often breaking up in the process into smaller chunks of rock.

When meteorites reach the surface of the Earth, they may crash intact, producing large craters like that found near Winslow Arizona, or they may break up in the air and form many smaller craters on impact. The crash may be heard hundreds of miles away. The largest known meteorite is in southern Africa, it weighs over 60 tonnes.

There are two kinds of meteorite, those formed of silicate rocks and those formed of iron. Both forms have a structure unlike anything comparable on Earth. They may be remnants of material from the original Solar System nebula or fragments from asteroids.

Index

Keep a record of your sightings by checking the boxes

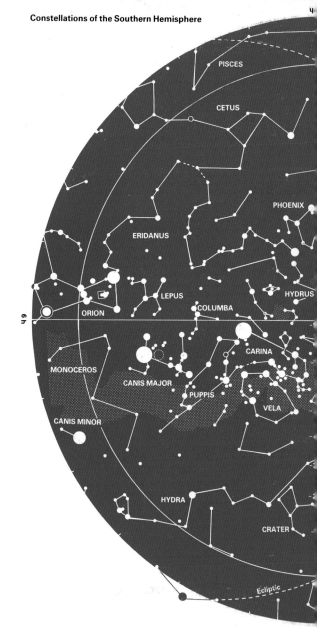

PISCES

CETUS

PHOENIX

ERIDANUS

LEPUS

HYDRUS

COLUMBA

ORION

CARINA

MONOCEROS

CANIS MAJOR

PUPPIS

VELA

CANIS MINOR

HYDRA

CRATER

Ecliptic